Tales of Old Worcestershire

Other Counties in this series include:

Tales of Old Worcestershire

Kathleen Lawrence-Smith

With Illustrations by Don Osmond

COUNTRYSIDE BOOKS
NEWBURY, BERKSHIRE

COUNTRYSIDE BOOKS
3 CATHERINE ROAD
NEWBURY, BERKSHIRE

ISBN 1 85306 051 8

Produced through MRM Associates, Reading
Typeset by Acorn Bookwork, Salisbury
Printed in England by J. W. Arrowsmith Ltd, Bristol

To my daughter, Veronica Naomi
whose vivid interest in the past
reawakened and stimulated my own

Acknowledgements

I am indebted to our County Records Office and the Staff of Worcester City Library for providing access to documents and books otherwise unavailable to me, including 'Portrait of An Obsession' by A. N. L. Munby (Constable, 1967), about the life of Sir Thomas Phillipps, R. Blunt's biography of the Second Lord Lyttelton (Putnam's Sons, N.Y., 1936), and Violet A. Wilson's book 'The Coaching Era' (Bodley Head, 1926).

Worcestershire is fortunate in its own past historians from whom I have learned much, and in its contemporary writers – H. W. Gwilliam who kindly allowed me to quote Thomas Pumphrey's birthday rhyme, Michael Craze, T.D., M.A., who shared information about the Gifford story; Barbara Middlemass and Joe Hunt who, in 'John Corbett, Pillar of Salt' encouraged my own view of that dynamic character. The Worcestershire Regiment supplied details about the exploit of Private Fred Dancox, V.C. My visit to Miss Cicely Lamb for the personal recollections of a lively 90-year-old villager, and Dr R. O. Walker's charming book on Witley Court and Church, both provided valuable insight into Great Witley's history.

Finally I warmly thank Nicholas Battle for inviting me to write this book. It was a challenge which I have much enjoyed.

Kathleen Lawrence-Smith

Contents

WORCESTERSHIRE – The map overleaf is by John Speede and shows the county as it was in the early seventeenth century.

Black Sheep
at the
Black Bull

THE ancient hostelry now known as The Old Bull at Inkberrow is the one on which the scriptwriter Godfrey Baseley based the Ambridge pub in the BBC radio programme *The Archers*. But the past history of The Old Bull proves that truth is often stranger than fiction. If some of the characters who actually lived in the village of Inkberrow and drank in this pub in centuries past were to be featured in the radio programme, they would seem unbelievable. Perhaps the most notorious of these was the young curate Edward Pearce, whose story has been traced by village historians Robert Hunt and Ruth Jackson in their book *Inkberrow Ways*.

In Edward Pearce's day the hostelry was known as The Black Bull and he must have been one of its most regular patrons around 1600. A popular parson is often depicted as one who will take a drink and mingle at the bar with his parishioners, but the Reverend Pearce's bonhomie went far beyond this. He was, in short, a thoroughly bad influence on village lads and a troublemaker among the whole community.

Old records describe him on one occasion sitting in the alehouse 'eating fresh herings', after which he went upstairs to his room to light a candle and place it in his bedroom window. This, he said, was the custom among students at Oxford when they wished to give the impression of being at work over their books while engaged on less commendable pursuits. On this particular night he was in the company of another fellow and two women and when they all decamped after placing the misleading signal, it is recorded that 'thereupon he and his companion in the night went abroad into the field with the two women very suspiciously'!

Pearce's favourite game, which he played for hours at the inn tables, was 'Fox Myne Host'. No details of its rules have come to light, but its title at least seems appropriate in view of the ruse with the candle. But later he seemed to become quite oblivious to the opinions of onlookers. He is described as having assaulted one Robert Twycross publicly in the bar because he suspected him of having reported his (the curate's) 'lewd behaviour.'

One November night Pearce set out with others on a bat-fowling expedition. These night flying creatures are capable of negotiating their way perfectly in dark woods and coppices. It is certain that the bat-hunters would need to have been quite sober to aim their fowling guns with any kind of precision! Maybe it was chagrin at their lack of success which prompted them to round off the expedition by setting fire to a field of corn, after which they dashed back to Inkberrow in high glee. Here they 'riotously drew drink into kettles' and set it to warm over the fire, with apples bobbing merrily in the brew!

It is satisfying to discover that justice caught up with the parson to some extent at the Quarter Sessions, where he was charged in 1602 as 'A Common Barrator, Caluminator, Cursar and stirer of the strife'. He may have had some knowledge of the law because it was his great glee to take out lawsuits against his neighbours, probably to intimidate them. In an effort to prevent Thomas Twycross (that family must have been plucky) from giving evidence against him, the curate obtained a letter of attorney to secure Thomas's arrest beforehand. He appears to have worked on the principle that offence is the best defence, but it is to be hoped that he did not get away with his abominable behaviour toward the landlady of one alehouse into which he dashed one day, imperiously demanding a drink. Because the woman did not immediately fly to his behest, he behaved detestably. Suffice it to say here that having damped down the fire in the hearth in a manner which cannot be described in polite society, he ended by dumping the poor landlady upon it!

The miscreants of the 18th century who patronised The Black Bull must have seemed quite tame in comparison. From time to time the hostelry provided unwanted lodgings for young men from neighbouring parishes who had been traced and apprehended for getting Inkberrow maidens into trouble. Village overseers took it upon their sturdy shoulders to lay a heavy hand upon their collars and bring them to lodge at The Black Bull until a marriage could be arranged. Their lodgings were paid for by the parish. The great aim of Poor Law administrators was to keep the rates down at all costs. It was cheaper to pay the bridegroom's lodgings at The Black Bull for a few nights than to risk maintaining a pauper child in Inkberrow for years to come!

It is rather engaging to find that The Black Bull provided the setting for teaching a man to face up to his domestic responsibilities. Ambridge's 'Mrs Perkins' would give the treatment her full approval.

The Jovial Hunter of Bromsgrove

FROM time immemorial a favourite tale for children and adults alike has been one which features a valiant rescuer delivering a helpless victim from the snare of a marauding beast. If the one at risk was a princess or a beautiful maiden, so much the better as it opened the way for valour, chivalry and romance. Just such an exciting set of characters and circumstances are combined in *The Ballad of Sir Ryalas, the Jovial Hunter of Bromsgrove*, which has served, in a lively and enjoyable way, to commemorate a legend associated with the Staffords of Grafton Manor, Bromsgrove.

During the 15th century a great area in North Worcestershire was covered by Feckenham Forest. Monarch oaks and towering beech trees threw out their gigantic branches unchecked, spreading a protective roof over the twisted undergrowth and fern below and providing cover for wolves, stags and fierce boars.

These dangerous and gloomy haunts provided the stage for the exploits of mighty hunters, after which they would return home to their manors and castles in triumph to celebrate their victories and display their trophies. Many a feast was begun by the triumphal display of a boar's head, and a popular host would be a lively fellow who would generously share both the trophies and the credit with his hunting companions. The

Jovial Hunter must, surely, have gained his reputation in just such a setting.

However, the exploit which is jubilantly commemorated in the ballad is the more remarkable because it was not performed in company during the thrill of the chase. Sir Ryalas was alone in the forest when he came upon a wild boar, which lay in wait to destroy all who passed that way. The boar, it is said, 'lived in an enchanted castle' and Sir Ryalas 'released from enchantment and the power of the boar a lady whom he afterwards married.'

Jabez Allies, a Worcestershire writer in the early 19th century brings the legend to a much more detailed and exciting climax in his book *Antiquities and Folklore of Worcestershire*, and quotes the ballad which he says was a favourite of natives of the forest. It runs:

> 'As I went up one brook, one brook –
> Well wind the horn, good hunter!
> I saw a maiden sit on a tree top,
> As thou art the jovial hunter.
>
> I said, fair maiden what brings you here?
> Well wind the horn, good hunter!
> It is the wild boar that has drove me here,
> As thou art the jovial hunter.'

At this point the hunter expresses a wish to see the wild boar. The winding of his horn, says the beautiful lady, will soon bring him out. And so it does. 'Whetting his tusks and crashing through the oak and ash' the boar springs into view before the jovial hunter. The ballad continues:

> 'They fought five hours one long summer's day –
> Well wind the horn, good hunter!
> Till the wild boar he yelled and he'd fain run away,
> And away from the jovial hunter.

Oh! Then he cut his head clean off –
Well wind the horn, good hunter!
Then there came an old lady running out of the wood,
Saying you have killed my pretty, my pretty spotted pig,
As thou art the jovial hunter.

Then at him, this old lady, she did go –
Well wind the horn, good hunter!
As he clove her from the top of her head to her toe,
That was killed by the jovial hunter.

In Bromsgrove church they both do lie –
Well wind the horn, good hunter!
There the wild boar is pictur'd by
Sir Ryalas, the jovial hunter.'

The inclusion of the old lady in the ballad would add a comic note, were it not for her gruesome fate. The reference to Bromsgrove church and the boar's head seems to confirm that the 'real' Sir Ryalas was indeed Sir Humphrey Stafford, who lived during the long reign of King Henry VI. The boar's head was a family crest and featured on the Bromsgrove tombs of that illustrious family who, more than once, played a part in English history.

Sir Humphrey was undoubtedly a hunting man, enjoying the patronage of the king and the privilege of the chase in Feckenham Forest, which bordered upon his own property of Grafton Manor. It may be that some notable exploit there inspired the legend and the ballad. But whether his success in winning the hand of Eleanor, daughter of Sir Thomas Aylesbury, was attended by danger or opposition from any powerful enemy or 'old lady' is not disclosed in the history books! The marriage was a very happy one. Then, while still in the prime of life, Sir Humphrey was called upon to face a new foe, with disastrous results.

In the high summer of 1450 Sir Humphrey and his brother William were summoned by the King's Council to leave their pleasant Worcestershire holdings and travel with all speed to

London. A horde of Kentish peasants were marching on the capital, led by Jack Cade, who represented himself to be a man of the people, risen to right their wrongs and injustices.

By the time they reached the southern outskirts of London, the horde had swelled to 10,000 men. They were met at Blackheath by the Staffords with the modest advance party supplied to them by the king, and confrontation flared into attack. The rebels made a show of retreating, then turned swiftly upon the pursuing army. For once, perhaps, Sir Humphrey lost his hunter's skill. The prey turned upon him in an unguarded moment – and by sheer weight of numbers Stafford's force was wiped out before King Henry could reach Blackheath with reinforcements.

The sight of the few pitiful refugees from Stafford's army so demoralised the king's force that it refused to fight. The Staffords had perished. Cade, swollen with pride, took the surrender wearing on his head Sir Humphrey's gold-studded brigandine with its Stafford crest. On 3rd July he had the effrontery to ride over London Bridge at the head of his jubilant followers, clad in the unmistakable armour of which Sir Humphrey had been so proud.

This devastating news must have been received with shock and horror by Lady Eleanor at Grafton Manor. Hopefully it gave her some consolation, a few days later, to hear that another defender had taken her husband's place, mustered an army at the Tower of London and, at the cost of thousands of lives, had overthrown the rebels.

Lady Eleanor lived on at Grafton Manor for another 30 years with her family, her eldest son (also named Humphrey) inheriting the title. During that time she founded a chantry in Bromsgrove church so that prayers might be said for the good estate of the king, the queen, herself and her late husband, together with their children. Shortly afterwards she was herself laid to rest there. Her effigy, alongside that of her husband, lies on a beautiful altar tomb on which Sir Humphrey's armour, stolen from his body by the rebels, has been restored to him, in stone. Though he lost his life in that last tremendous challenge at Blackheath, he would have sold it dearly, and while the legend and the ballad remain Worcestershire folk will salute him still:

'Well wind the horn, good hunter!'

The Bird
of Ill Omen

HAGLEY HALL is still home to the descendants of the Lytteltons, a family which has contributed greatly to the life of the nation as well as to Worcestershire. In 1760 George Lyttleton, the 5th baronet, was so impatient to show off the beautiful Hall he had built to replace the damp, decaying Elizabethan manor house which had served past generations, that some overnight guests complained afterwards of having slept in damp beds!

The family saga which revolved around the tense relationship between father and son in the late 18th century was to become a very public affair, for George Lyttelton was a national figure. He had been private secretary to the Prince of Wales and later served in the government as Chancellor of the Exchequer. Because he spent so much time in the capital and travelling with the Prince, he did not get to know his children well until his retirement from state affairs and his elevation to the peerage. Sadly, the children had been deprived also of the influence of their mother. She died when young Tom was only three years old and little Lucy, his sister, was barely two.

George Lyttelton took his growing son on a tour of Scotland and was delighted to detect considerable gifts in him – wit, personality and a surprisingly shrewd awareness of national and world affairs for one so young. As they visited friends and relatives in the north, the father's pride was unbounded. He prophesied a brilliant future for his son in line with the

Lyttelton tradition. If Tom enjoyed his father's approbation at the time, he was later to look back upon it with resentment. He had been placed upon a pedestal. His balance thereon became altogether too precarious.

But it was almost certainly the Grand Tour which, in George Lyttelton's eyes, established the rift between himself and Tom. His lively, quick-witted son was then 19 years old, just out of university and about to 'broaden his mind' by travel. By the time he had crossed the Alps into Turin he was writing home that he found the ladies 'handsome', the gaming tables even more beguiling, and the wines delectable! He returned to England with a taste for high living, strong wine and bad company – and to spend more time at the family's town house than in the peaceful Hagley countryside.

Then, for a while, the old peer's hopes revived. Tom was elected to represent Bewdley, a few miles from Hagley, as their Member of Parliament – a result, no doubt, of the family's status in the county. Once again Lord Lyttelton could revel in the wit, eloquence and surprising authority which his son displayed on the floor of the House. Then, alas, Tom's election victory was challenged, his narrow margin reversed, and the seat awarded to a rival candiate. Frustrated, and soon bored with country life again, Tom returned to clubs, bars, theatres, coffee houses and venues of even more doubtful reputation. The old fondness for wine and bad company set the seal upon a way of life which distanced him from his father.

Tom Lyttelton was in Paris on the September day in 1773 when he received news of his father's death. For ten years past that relationship had been stormy. Attempts at reconciliation had constantly ended in failure and in Tom seeking refuge from bitter reproaches by escaping to the Continent. The last escapade in which he had been involved, and the reason for his present absence from the English scene, had been widely reported in the Press and the London journals. It was known to have caused his father great distress. It was unfortunate that the peson with whom he picked a quarrel was also editor of *The Morning Post*!

In the past year, however, things might not have been so bad if it had not been for the problem of Apphia! Tom's father had welcomed his son's marriage, 15 months earlier, to Apphia Peach, a young widow with a small fortune who had recently returned from India to live in nearby 'Leasowes'. Tom happened to be in Hagley at that time. He had rushed Mrs Peach into marriage rather too soon for good taste in polite society, but Lord Lyttelton had been so relieved at this sign of felicity (Tom seemed genuinely taken with the young widow) that he opened his home and heart to the young couple. But scarcely had he completed his round of letter writing announcing his confidence in Tom's reform, than the impulsive bridegroom had absconded – in all probability into the arms of Alicia Dawson, the one woman who seemed able to hold his affections!

When Tom returned to England after his father's death he reached Hagley to find his usual ground floor suite prepared for him. Soon he was conferring with his father's brothers and burial arrangements were completed. It probably was no surprise to Tom to discover that his father had left a debt of £26,000 on the estate. The building and furnishing of Hagley Hall had been the late peer's pride and joy; no expense had been spared. Tom's father had often pleaded poverty when refusing to increase his son's £500 a year allowance. When reproached for gambling Tom had often claimed that had it not been for his success at the gaming tables he could not have existed this past ten years. It was ironic that he was now called upon to tackle the financial strain left on the Hagley estate by his estimable parent!

The newly elevated peer could not then have had the slightest inkling that he had only six years in which to prove himself to the world around him. Wandering through the beautiful rooms which were now his for his lifetime, Tom must have felt some latent pride in recognising that his father's vision, dedication and good taste had produced one of the most outstanding achievements of the century. As he valued the contents for probate, the family portraits alone would speak to him of past glories.

Having dealt with immediate affairs at Hagley, Tom set off for the town house in Hill Street, from where he intended to take up his Parliamentary career. He had first to 'buy out' Apphia, who had been left the right of occupation there for a period. Tom's good intentions do not appear to have included any attempt at a reconciliation with his wife and she returned to Worcestershire. But Tom's record in the House of Lords between 1773 and 1779 was exemplary. He showed a marked perception of British and world affairs. He recognised the fallacy of continuing the War of Independence with the American rebels two years before England ended hostilities. Tom deeply deplored the loss to England. His logic was clear and eloquent.

Sadly, he did not carry the same wisdom back with him to Hill Street. The London scene still beckoned him. He played host to a succession of disreputable characters, countering reproof by saying that his former reputation denied him access to better companions. The kind of company he kept could be enjoyed without the strain of odious comparisons! Even so, he became a rake plagued with a conscience.

On the night of 24th November 1779, a very disturbing event occurred. Around midnight Tom had a strange dream in his Hill Street bedroom – or assumed it to be a dream. It seemed to him that he was in a room into which a bird flew and that the bird turned into a woman, clothed in white, who bade him prepare to die. His answer was: 'I hope not soon, not in two months,' to which the strange visitor replied: 'Yes, in three days,' and vanished into the night.

He recounted the dream at breakfast next morning to his guests, but did not appear unduly disturbed. He dressed with his usual care, departed for the House of Lords and became immersed in the current debate on the troubles in Ireland. Several experienced Parliamentarians were convinced that Tom Lyttelton's star was in the ascendancy, that he was on the verge of fame and a sphere of influence in national affairs.

But it was not to be. This was the 36 year old peer's last speech. He returned to Hill Street and arranged to take his guests down to his country house for the weekend. Seeing some trepidation on the face of one guest, he assured her that he 'had lived two days and God willing I will live out the third!'

On the Saturday morning Tom summoned his coachman and the party reached Pitt Place. To add cheer to what could turn out to be an anxious evening, a musician was engaged to play the pianoforte in the anteroom adjoining the drawing room. Here the party, reinforced by a number of local guests, assembled after enjoying a good dinner. Tom had eaten heartily and declared himself well. The pianist played on, noting lively conversation and bursts of laughter in the next room. He had been booked until midnight, but shortly after eleven o'clock the host came to him, 'paid him handsomely' and invited him to partake of supper before leaving. For some reason the clocks at Pitt Place were running an hour fast, so that when Tom retired after bidding the musician goodnight, he and others in the household seem to have thought it already past midnight.

According to Tom's valet, who accompanied him to the bedroom, his master was quite cheerful and ordered breakfast rolls for the morrow. Why should he not be happy – he had survived the third, fatal day of his dream. He sat upon the side of the bed. The man was in the process of pulling off Tom's waistcoat when Tom clutched his side, sank back upon the bed, and expired in the arms of the valet!

Thus abruptly ended the chequered career of the 2nd Lord Lyttelton, his death as great an enigma as his life. His physician ascribed it to a burst blood vessel. Others spoke of brain haemorrhage or possibly heart failure, the effect of the dream upon an excitable disposition perhaps? Who, or what else could have been responsible? Perhaps only the bird of ill omen could tell!

The King and the Waggoner

THE waggoner hitched up his horse and dray on the morning of 3rd September 1651, and set out from Elmley Castle to join the Worcester road at Pershore. Under cloudless skies, John Moore made his peaceful progress on what seemed an idyllic day, to bring his load of hay to market in Worcester. But as he neared the city's outlying villages, he was arrested by the first faint sounds of musket shot and cannon fire. Presently the clash of steel and iron, and the shrill cries of men and horses, alerted Moore to the realisation that this was no mere sporadic foray. This was a battle, widespread and in deadly earnest. What had seemed earlier to be little more than romantic rumour had come to pass. Charles Stuart had come to Worcester, well known for its Royalist sympathies in the past, to reclaim his father's throne.

The Elmley Castle villager encountered others along the Pershore to Worcester road and paused to exchange news and check the situation ahead of him, but he continued doggedly on. Home was ten or twelve miles behind him so his hopes were pinned on being admitted inside the city wall to find shelter, along with his merchandise, in the premises of his customer. Hopefully that citizen was not involved with the battle raging around the city! Local tradesmen, Moore hoped, could pursue their normal business with sensible caution.

Worcester was thronged with horses and riders. The city would need the waggoner's hay, whoever prevailed in battle. A man had to be practical!

As Moore picked his way downhill toward the city gate he learned that the Battle of Worcester was going against the Cavaliers. Cromwell's vastly superior forces, 30,000 in all, had successfully operated a pincer movement around the Royalists, who had mustered little more than half that number. Unfortunately for Charles, promised reinforcements had failed to arrive. And even the 16,000 men under Charles's command were disunited – the Scots and the English were far from fraternal. Some valiant fighting and flashes of success by individual officers and men could not prevail against such odds indefinitely.

In the late afternoon of that warm September day, as Moore approached the city entrance, the moment of reckoning had come for Charles Stuart. He was urged to flee the scene of conflict whilst his supporters tried to hold off Cromwell's men. Just as Moore reached the city gate, he all but collided with the escaping King, who sped through the gateway on foot, his horse having been shot from under him. A party of Parliamentarians were in hot pursuit only a few hundred yards away. The quick witted waggoner thrust his cart across the gateway and, according to some reports, upended it and tipped its load into the roadway. The entrance was blocked, and gave the King a few vital moments of respite from his pursuers. Before the haycart could be dragged aside from the gateway, the King had regained his balance and was looking swiftly round for his next move.

Hopefully Moore, stumbling through the overturned hay, had the satisfaction of seeing the Sidbury brewer, William Bagnall, thrust forward his own horse for the King to leap into the saddle. Thus began one of the most famous escapes in English history.

Charles sped through Friar Street and on into the Cornmarket where his temporary headquarters lay – the black and white gabled house which now bears his name in the city. By happy circumstance (or Providence) the house possessed an exit opening on to the road which skirted the city wall. Just as the Roundheads reached the front door of the house, the King hurtled through the back exit and disappeared at top speed for the northern outskirts of the city.

Via Ombersley, Hartlebury and Stourbridge, Charles rode in zigzag fashion across the county, before crossing the border into the Black Country. Legends abound of his narrow escapes, concealed at times of imminent danger in an oak tree or a chimney breast, or riding behind Jane Lane on horseback and in various disguises. It must, though, have been an ignominious flight, overcast with fear, and a sense of failure and the knowledge that many were left behind to pay a heavy price for their adherence to his cause.

It is a strange irony that on a day of magnificent endeavour in battle, with sacrifices and acts of heroism involving the cream of the Scottish aristocracy and some Englishmen of high rank, it was the quick action of a simple villager which saved Charles Stuart and launched him on the great escape which preserved his life and eventually provided the English throne with one of its most colourful characters. It is good to know that the King, on his return to England in 1660, was told the tale of Moore's deed. He rewarded the villager with the gift of a farm at Kersoe, adjoining Elmley Castle, parts of which still remain, including the timbered beams of the farmhouse itself and its ancient floorboards. Elmley Castle continues to celebrate Oak Apple Day (commemorating the restoration of Charles II to the throne) to this day.

The Rejected Princess

BRIHTRIC MEAW must have appeared to be the obvious choice when King Edward the Confessor looked for an ambassador to represent him at the court of Baldwin, the powerful Count of Flanders, in the middle of the 11th century. Nobly-born, handsome and wealthy, only the king himself was richer than Brihtric, whose happiest years were spent at his hunting lodge in the forest-covered plain between the Malvern Hills and the river Severn, near the ford of Hanley. The vast estates that he had inherited from his grandfather, Haylward, stretched beyond the Severn and southwards down to Cornwall.

Both Brihtric's father and grandfather had distinguished themselves in past years, battling valiantly against the marauding Danes on the Worcestershire border. Now the Danes had gone, an English king was on the throne, and during this interval of blessed peace came the opportunity of an important diplomatic role for the young Brihtric.

On the face of it, this mission on the Continent presented little danger. But danger there was, and it sprang, not from ill will or from concealed enmity at the court of Flanders, but from the passionate, stubborn love of a beautiful 14 year old girl. According to the historian Salt Brassington, 'When the young ambassador arrived in Flanders his noble carriage and manly beauty attracted great attention, and Matilda, Princess of Flanders, fell madly in love with him.'

It was not unusual for girls of Matilda's age, or even younger, to be betrothed. This was often arranged for political reasons, and there is little doubt that the princess's father would have welcomed the liaison with Brihtric. But for some reason (perhaps loyalty to an earlier attachment?) the young nobleman held back from the dazzling prospect of marrying into the house of Flanders, which was exceedingly powerful and influential throughout Europe.

It was a pity that the young princess had not inherited her father's restrained disposition. 'Passion triumphed over modesty,' says Brassington, 'and the haughty princess revealed the love which a humbler maiden would have concealed.' How the blond young Englishman managed to extricate himself from this difficult situation we can only guess at. What is certain however, is that Brihtric lived to regret his rejection of the princess of Flanders.

Brihtric returned home to England and was quite content to take up his role as the Lord of Hanley, and to develop his vast inherited estates in the south west. Meanwhile, during the seven years which followed his mission to Flanders, Matilda steadfastly refused all offers of marriage, including that from her father's powerful neighbour, Duke William of Normandy. He, however, was as stubborn as she was, and persisted, at intervals, in sending his envoys to the Count of Flanders to pursue his suit. Finally Matilda retorted that not only did she love another man, but that she would never accept the proposal of a bastard!

Although he had been openly acknowledged as the son of Duke Robert of Normandy, it was ever a source of embarrassment to William that his father's liaison with Arlotta, the daughter of a tanner in Falaise, had fallen short of the marriage tie. When news reached him of Matilda's insulting rejection and of her contemptuous allusion to his birth, his outrage knew no bounds. He threw diplomacy to the winds. Saddling a fast horse, he rode furiously to Bruges. As the princess emerged with her ladies from the peaceful sanctity of the cathedral after mass, she was astonished to be confronted by her enraged suitor. Action spoke louder than words – he grabbed her by the hair, beat her about the body and shoulders, then thrust her to the ground to be rolled in the muddy gutter and drenched with rainwater! He then turned on his heel, mounted his waiting charger and rode away without a backward glance.

The sequel to this peremptory manhandling was equally astonishing. The princess's father was incensed at the sight of his bruised and bedraggled daughter returning from mass, and summoned his neighbour of Normandy to the court of Flanders – only to be astounded when Matilda spoke up for herself to the assembled company and declared her willingness to become William's wife! The shrew had succumbed. A splendid marriage took place almost immediately and the pair won admiration and acclaim wherever they went in a triumphal procession through William's territories in Normandy.

What Brihtric Meaw thought of this strange turn of events is not easy to imagine. If he heaved a sigh of relief, it was sadly premature. For in 1066 the Duke of Normandy invaded England and earned himself the title by which he was to go down into history – The Conqueror.

Whether Brihtric took up arms with King Harold against Duke William at Hastings in that fateful September is not clear. But defeat and enemy occupation, which now faced England, presents an inevitable risk to existing landowners, even where there is no personal axe to grind. Any conquering ruler, establishing a new regime, will want to reward his followers while subjugating defenders of the old order. A penalty for the one provides a prize for the other.

For Brihtric Meaw, whose association with Normandy was a delicate one, the hour of reckoning came, ironically, on a day of celebration. He had just completed the building of a chapel for his tenants and retainers. The famous St Wulstan had hallowed the chapel and scarcely had the guests risen from the festal board when mail-clad Norman soldiers clattered into the courtyard of the manor and arrested the Lord of Hanley. He was then hurried, says an ancient chronicler, 'from the forest glades of Worcestershire to a noisome prison in faraway Winchester.' His possessions were confiscated and presented to none other than the new Queen Matilda!

The Domesday Book records this sober fact and suggests that Brihtric's fate was sealed because of his past unfortunate encounter with the lovelorn Matilda. There is a clear inference that he was the victim of the new Queen's revenge. But she had been happily married for more than 14 years and contemporary writers were expressing admiration of her outstanding qualities of judgement and benevolence. It is therefore more than possible that William himself was the source of his old rival's humiliation and tragedy. This award to Matilda may have been intended by the mighty Duke as a recompense to her for past slights, or, perhaps, to establish, once and for all, William's own supremacy over the handsome young nobleman who had once dominated the affections of Matilda of Flanders.

Brihtric did not live long to reflect on these weighty matters. While the Conqueror and Matilda went on to establish their great role in England's history, he died in his miserable prison and was privately buried – a heavy price to pay for that rejected love!

Comrades
Under Fire

L ADY MABELLE EGERTON'S splendid canteen, created out
of a huge shed in a railway siding in Rouen, provided a
brief home-from-home for British Tommies in the First World
War. Awaiting dispersal over the battlefields, many of them
were mere boys on their first trip abroad with only the vaguest
idea as to what awaited them in the coming days. Lady
Mabelle's canteen was a godsend.

So, too, in perhaps a more literal sense of that word, was the
lively, friendly little padre who came alongside the train to
greet each new contingent. He was Geoffrey Studdert Kennedy, who had left his vicarage in a poor Worcester parish to
join the men. He was himself a staunch patriot and had
unhesitatingly preached from St Paul's pulpit that every able-
bodied man should volunteer to play his part in the war. A
firm believer in practising what he preached, he had prevailed
upon his Bishop to find a replacement at St Paul's while he
did his duty on the Western Front.

For several months he was under orders to serve in this
reception and dispersal point at Rouen. After entertaining the
troops by singing songs from home, he won their confidence
and received rapt attention when he dropped into a man-to-
man talk on deeper matters. Letters home, he would tell the
men, were invaluable. But he knew what a chore it was to put
pen to paper and volunteered to do the job for them. Men
would crowd around him with names and addresses scribbled

on grubby bits of paper, and they even entrusted him with crumpled ten shilling or pound notes to pop in as personal gifts and tokens of love.

All too soon would come their summons to entrain for the Front and the padre would follow them onto the train with two heavy packs on his shoulders. Up and down the compartments he would move, rapidly handing out New Testaments, other literature and the little pale green packs of cigarettes which earned for him the name which would never be forgotten in Worcester, or indeed throughout the length and breadth of England – 'Woodbine Willie'.

Then came the call for which Studdert Kennedy had waited for months – to proceed to the Front and to experience at first hand the trauma, the terror and the tyranny of warfare. He took part in the Somme offensive in June 1916 and discovered that he was not of that dauntless brigade who feel no fear. A year later he took part in the attack on the Messines Ridge. Army records describe this as a bitter and disheartening time. Kennedy found himself tending heavy casualties at a time when morphia supplies ran out. In the face of such need, he set off to fetch fresh stocks from another station over ground that was being heavily shelled. It meant dropping into shell holes for cover in between making a series of zigzag spurts, but he returned bearing the precious painkiller. Outside on the open ground lay three wounded men, and for these he returned, dodging more missiles. He managed to save two of them but their comrade, stumbling behind him, was brought down by a screaming shell. This was the day, in the summer of 1917, when he won his Military Cross 'for conspicuous gallantry and devotion to duty.'

A telephone call shortly afterwards summoned him to leave the field of conflict for a brief leave home in Worcester and to receive his award. People at home were avid for news from the Front, and though the brutality of war now appalled him, he did what he could to comfort the families who flocked around him.

It is probable that Ellen Dancox was among those who came to seek news. Her home was less than a quarter of a mile from the padre's vicarage. Her husband was fighting in the same theatre of war which he had just left. Private Frederick Dancox of the 4th Battalion The Worcestershire Regiment had so far survived three years of soldiering. It was when the Army was approaching Passchendaele that the resourcefulness of Fred Dancox made history. Suddenly he found himself alone, in front, within 200 yards of the machine-gun emplacement which had destroyed comrades all around him. With what his regiment described later as 'cool courage' this intrepid soldier stumbled forward, dodging from one shell hole to another, and ran the gauntlet of bursting shells from his own side. Miraculously he worked his way around to the rear of the concrete pillbox housing the machine-gun, and sprang into the midst of the astonished Germans, brandishing a Mills bomb in his right hand.

The enemy immediately surrendered! The Worcester man backed out of the doorway signalling them to follow him to the Allied lines, but paused just long enough to grab the machine-gun. His return to his own ranks with one unused bomb, one enemy machine-gun and 40 unresisting prisoners was greeted with hilarious cheers. It was a tonic such as they had never hoped for – a couragious reconnoitre that brought almost comic relief – and brought the reward of a well earned Victoria Cross for Private Dancox.

Sadly, Fred did not live to receive his award in person. Fred Dancox was killed at the Battle of Cambrai, on the very day he should have been returning home on leave. His reception party had already assembled at Shrub Hill station when the sickening news arrived.

The tide of war turned at last and Studdert Kennedy returned to his Worcester parish, but he never forgot those war-time comrades and commemorated them in many ways. His Kipling-style verse in soldier-dialect was very appealing. *A Sermon in a Billet* contains the lines:

'There's nuthin in man that's perfect,
And nuthin' that's all complete;
'E's nubbut a big beginning
From 'is 'ead to the soles of 'is feet.
There's summut 'as draws 'im uppards,
And summut 'as drags 'im down,
And the consekence is, 'e wobbles
'Twixt muck and a golden crown . . ..'

Fred Dancox's widow received his posthumous award with pride, but was left to cope with bringing up her four children in poverty. 'Woodbine Willie' continued to 'fight the good fight' in his Worcester parish after the war and became nationally-known for his selfless dedication. The two men, Worcester heroes both, were so different. One was a slight, studious, sad-eyed man, a little comical in appearance, it is said, but with a lively tongue and a ready pen. And the other was a tall, well-built man who had been a toiler in the open air, a hay-cutter and a good, solid family man who never thought to make history. Yet he was the only Worcester VC and left behind a legendary tale of derring-do, a brand of individual, unrehearsed heroism performed with a nonchalance that would have done credit to a superman.

The Warrior Queen

O N Saturday, 4th May 1471, while the Battle of Tewkesbury raged in the meadow below his mansion house,
Thomas Payne, wool merchant, was startled by a frantic
beating upon his door. There he found an exhausted, mud-
stained group – Queen Margaret, her 16 year old daughter-in-
law, Anne of Warwick, and several agitated attendants. The
party had fled from savage hand-to-hand fighting on the
battlefield to make for Little Malvern Priory, six or seven
miles away, intending there to wait, watch and pray for the
outcome of the battle.

To all intents and purposes this was to be the last drama in
the Wars of the Roses – the long struggle between the rival
Dukes of York and of Lancaster to occupy England's throne.
On this fateful day in 1471 Edward of York was in power,
reigning as Edward IV, while Margaret's husband, Henry
VI, had been deposed and was imprisoned in the Tower of
London. Now Margaret and her son Edward were fighting
back in a desperate attempt to regain the throne for the House
of Lancaster. The 42 year old French-born queen, one of the
most fascinating and dynamic women of her time, had gained
a formidable reputation as a commander and strategist on the
battlefield.

It so happened that there was a right of way through the

great hall of Payne's Place in the village of Bushley, the home which Thomas had built for his family 20 years earlier. Hurriedly the request was made for the fugitives to cross the hall and leave by the opposite door to find a trackway to Malvern Chase. But then Margaret paused in the headlong rush and impulsively asked the good merchant and his wife Ursula that she be allowed to stay here, within sight and sound of the battle, while her companions sped on ahead to the priory. It was after all only for the protection of her young daughter-in-law, who (if all went well with Prince Edward) would be a future Queen of England, that the women had left the battle.

The Paynes did not hesitate. Gratefully the Queen accepted the offer of the bedroom on the eastern wing, overlooking the field of conflict and the grey tower of Tewkesbury Abbey beyond it. She would not be deterred from the grim spectacle, the clash of steel and iron, the twang of the archer's bow, the terrified neighing of horses, the yelled commands, the shouting and anguished cries of fear and pain. Only with reluctance had she left the scene and yielded command.

Downstairs the Paynes strove to preserve an air of normality. They must have known that by taking in the Queen they were in some peril, so it was safer that no one else should be aware of their unexpected guest. Seated at the long table in the great hall, master and mistress at the head, children and servants at the lower end, the family took their repast as usual.

News filtered through from the battlefield from time to time and long before nightfall it was clear that the fighting was virtually over. The Lancastrians were in flight! Hundreds had perished on the field. Some had drowned in their heavy armour, trying to cross the river. Others had fled for sanctuary to Tewkesbury Abbey. Even in that sacred place many had been killed as they crouched in the aisles or side chapels.

So it was grim news that the Paynes had to convey to their stricken guest upstairs, though the outcome must already have been obvious to her trained eye. Soon her anguished mind could concentrate only on the possible fate of her son.

Conflicting reports drifted in from the town over the county border. He had been slain on the battlefield ... had died of wounds ... had fled to abbey sanctuary. If so – had he died there by sword or a dagger thrust? Or was he among the few survivors at the altar who the scandalized priests had managed to defend? Later it was claimed by some vigilant observer that he had been seen to surrender to a Yorkist knight on the field and taken captive into the presence of the conquering Edward of York and his brothers, the Dukes of Clarence and of Gloucester.

For Queen Margaret that prospect would have been the worst. In like circumstances she herself had shown little mercy to the vanquished foe. What mercy could Prince Edward expect now? These grave misgivings must have been shared during the long night vigil by the Queen with her hosts. The Paynes had little comfort or reassurance to offer. They themselves were in some danger, yet they had no thought of protecting their interests by betraying the Queen.

On the following morning Thomas and most of his family put in an appearance at Bushley church. They heard that 16 officers of the army of the red rose were still in sanctuary. But on the day following – a black Monday morning in Tewkesbury – King Edward's promise of safe conduct was broken. As soon as the 16 emerged from sanctuary they were arrested, brought to a hasty trial and summarily executed on an improvised scaffold set up in the town centre. Margaret may have drawn a crumb of comfort from confirmation that Prince Edward was not among them at the last. It is said that his defiant and courageous response under interrogation by the victors had met with a dagger-thrust and swift death in comparative privacy.

Nothing now remained for the Queen to fight for. With her son dead and her husband imprisoned, the only concern now was to cope with her present danger and that into which she had put her generous host. Even so, the Paynes pressed her to stay another night under their roof while King Edward's scouts were scouring the countryside for her. On the next morning, Tuesday 7th May, Thomas saddled his mare and took the Queen, seated behind him for better concealment, to Malvern Priory where he bade her farewell.

Next day the Paynes were saddened to hear that Lord Stanley had arrested Queen Margaret, and had taken her to Worcester and to King Edward. She escaped death, but was taken by the king's retinue to London. As the procession entered the streets of the capital she was openly mocked as she went to the Tower to join King Henry. It is likely that the Paynes heaved a sigh of relief when her cousin the King of France ransomed her for 50,000 crowns three years after Tewkesbury's battle. She died in her 50s, desolate and impoverished.

The years were kinder to Thomas and Ursula Payne. Trade flourished and markets in England and in France increased. Seven sons and four daughters eventually completed the family at Payne's Place, where they lived in contentment among the parishioners of Bushley. Six years after Tewkesbury's battle the sturdy, honest wool clothier was commended for his 'unwearied efforts' to obtain permission 'to bury the bodies of the faithful' in Bushley church and graveyard.

To that same quiet country churchyard Thomas Payne himself came to rest in the year 1500. Though the church has since been demolished and rebuilt, the Paynes' brass memorial still survives, showing the couple in voluminous 15th century costume. The memorial to Thomas and Ursula concludes with the gentle prayer 'To whose souls may God be merciful.' If it is true that mercy begets mercy, the Paynes' selfless hospitality in those epic days and nights in 1471 will have reaped their just reward.

The
Salt King
of Droitwich

IF only John Corbett had been born with a sense of humour, or at least with some degree of geniality in his disposition, all might have been so different for this Black Country bargee who brought prosperity to the little town of Droitwich in the mid 1850s.

The British Rock & Patent Salt Company and its rivals, Fardon's Salt & Alkali Works, had enjoyed several years of prosperity, sinking their great shafts into the earth to locate and bring up the salty liquid. After bringing the brine to the surface by a laborious pumping method it was channelled into a kind of distillery, heated to boiling point in metal pans and maintained at high temperatures. Then the salt crystals could be raked to the sides of the huge steaming vats by perspiring men and women under appalling conditions – sweated labour in the truest sense. Every ton of salt produced demanded heat generated by half a ton of coal. Corbett, with his enquiring mind and observant eye, must have watched the process when delivering coal to the works or collecting salt for the markets, for when the salt crystals were extracted, cooled off and the molten mass shaped to a convenient size, the salt blocks were ready for his collection. But the process was laborious and costs began to mount. The

industry was dying, and eventually The Alkali companies went into liquidation.

A champion now rose to the industry's cause. John Corbett purchased part of the site, six acres of derelict land, for a little over £1,000. He knew how to learn by other men's mistakes. From some years spent as an apprentice at a Brierley Hill ironworks, John knew that iron could be moulded and manipulated to form a sleeve inside the mining shafts, protecting them against seepage and ensuring that the rich brine in the well below could be raised without dilution. Now in his mid 30s, the new proprietor rose to the challenge and sank everything he had, his knowledge, energy, hopes and powers of persuasion into his enterprise. It was an almost superhuman endeavour. Very few would back him. But soon he had taken over the remaining mines and restored the industry single-handed.

He was a workaholic and a businessman with a sharp eye to economic management, yet he deplored the conditions in which his employees were forced to exist on the site. They occupied shacks little better than hovels. Both sexes slaved in the sweltering foetid atmosphere, half clothed or not at all, and lived with scant respect for the niceties of the marriage tie. Corbett, an Anglican churchgoer with a conscience, changed all that. According to Salt Brassington (a contemporary of John Corbett) in his *Historic Worcestershire*, 'Owing to the philanthropic spirit of John Corbett, Esq. . . . female labour in the salt works has been abolished.' No record appears of the said female labour fighting for their lost status. Perhaps the proprietor's provision of decent terraced houses with amenities above the norm for that day, and the raising of men's wages to compensate for the wives' lost paypackets, made all the difference.

At this point John might well have sat back and been satisfied, but a trip to France in search of markets led him to Paris, to Anna O'Meara and to an exciting and unpredictable romance. The O'Mearas were an Irish family of some distinction and Corbett's host, William, was attached to the Diplomatic Corps and lived with his wife, Adele, and two daughters in the French capital. William O'Meara looked quite favourably upon the rather uncultured Englishman who came under the spell of his eldest daughter.

Returning home to Stoke Prior, John must have rejoiced at his good fortune. Stoke Grange, two miles from his works, was a pleasant country house and the prospect of bringing to it a dazzling, lively girl of such contrasting background to his own, must have been a thrilling one. Within twelve months he returned to Paris to claim his bride, dismissing at the time the possible obstacle to happiness presented by her Roman Catholicism. John was a staunch Anglican with an antipathy, quite common in those days, to all 'popery'. But bringing Anna away from her family and the French influence, he possibly thought to win her over to joining him at St Michael's, Stoke Prior's parish church. He married Anna in Paris and returned home in some triumph to present the dainty 25 year old mistress of Stoke Grange to her waiting domestic staff. The year of this new beginning was 1856. John Corbett was 39 years old.

The next 20 years were momentous ones. Anna presented John with two sons and three daughters. The business prospered and was enlarged to the point where Corbett could build his own boats and wagons to bring in the huge coal stocks and to take out his finished product to customers around England. He began to husband his resources for investment in other industries. And with it all he maintained a flow of goodwill by his generosity to many good causes. Then his horizon widened to take in the world of politics. If he could succeed in business, improve the lot of workers and fellow citizens, why not exert influence in government? He joined the Liberal party and made his first bid for Parliament in 1868.

His initial defeat, after a hard and acrimonious battle did not deter John Corbett from a second attempt. He began preparations, it seems, by planning a far more imposing home base from which to fight for recognition. Undoubtedly the dream house was Anna's inspiration, from the beautiful chateaux along the Loire Valley. The first step was to acquire the manor of Impney, two miles from Droitwich along the Birmingham road.

And so began that second enterprise with which John Corbett was to leave his mark in Droitwich history – the long, costly but vastly exciting project of raising up a magnificent chateau in the English countryside. Down came the manor house, though with elaborate care so that it could be reconstructed elsewhere, and the 200 acre site formed the setting for the leading French architect's magnificent plan. The result (unique in England) has been described as an enchanted palace, supporting towers and turrets of beautiful proportions and design. The edifice was raised in English brick and stone but skilled workers from the Continent were summoned to fashion the plasterwork, such an important factor in the interior fabrication. Hundreds of workmen swarmed through the grounds in the years that followed, and the ambitious project was fulfilled in every small detail exactly as planned.

The windows opened on to a vista of well laid out gardens, fountains springing from pools of clear water and a variety of ornamental stone statues placed at strategic intervals. In the grounds, too, was built an ice house for food storage, and a heated grotto to house exotic plants and fruits. Two lodges of chateau-like design flanked the magnificent wrought iron entrance gates. Not surprisingly work was provided for 40 gardeners to maintain at high standard hundreds of trees and plants, and to ensure the clear flow of the little river Salwarpe, winding its way through the grounds to connect up with the appropriately named 'Salty Brook'.

Obviously this great project took several years to accomplish. In fact, the next General Election overtook its completion. This time John Corbett made a striking victory at the polls over the titled landowner who had held the seat for 37 years! With another ambition realised, and with the pleasant task of selecting beautiful furnishings, pictures, objets d'art and a variety of antique pieces, 1875 was a busy year, culminating in the move of the Corbett family into Chateau Impney.

It would be a splendid thing if it could be recorded that in this fairytale palace everyone lived happily ever after. Alas, this was very far from the true situation. Later events were to prove that despite his great achievements, his philanthropy and indeed his close personal attention to many causes, the father of the family was not loved by his nearest and dearest. The word 'humourless' crops up again and again in descriptions of his demeanour which was in marked contrast to Anna's lively disposition. Inevitably clashes of personality occurred beneath the blue ceilings and the moulded cherubs! The children drew closer to their mother. John became isolated.

If the provision of that beautiful home had been designed to improve his standing with Anna and the children, it failed abysmally. Their home life seems to have maintained a reasonable appearance, but the family rarely supported him publicly at the many functions he performed or attended. And through all those 20 years of marriage there remained the considerable obstacle of their differing religious views. The new home gave Anna easier access to the Catholic church and she received frequent home visits from her Father Confessor. John's own religious observances had to be taken alone, like most of his other pursuits, business, social or political.

Then came the death blow to any hopes of conjugal happiness. In the year following the move to the chateau Anna gave birth to a sixth child, a daughter, in the smaller of the two main bedrooms. John, aghast at this (to him) unexpected arrival, was roused to fury. He had occupied a separate room for several years. The last Corbett child, he declared, was the son born nine years before. Who could be responsible? There could not have been too many candidates for suspicion. He became convinced that the visits of the Father Confessor had not been purely for the good of Anna's soul!

It probably seemed a godsend when John Corbett heard that the manor of Ynysymaengwen, a 15 acre estate in the Cardigan Bay area of the Welsh coast, was on the market. The little town welcomed the new squire and his lady with some ceremony, quite unaware of the unfolding domestic drama which was heading for an official separation. Ynys provided a home for Anna, John remaining at the chateau.

The long, solitary years at Droitwich and Stoke Prior continued to be marked by the same enterprise and benevolence for which John had an established reputation. Several buildings, including the birthplace of St Richard de Wych, were bought up, renovated, refurbished and opened as splendid hotels to accommodate the growing number of visitors to the little town, which was now developing into a spa through the added attraction of the brine baths. It is true they were not Corbett's brainchild. It is said that the health-giving properties were discovered accidentally, either by a worker falling into the hot brine, or by a pailful of hot brine being thrown into the bath of a cholera patient during one fearful epidemic. His recovery apparently was quite dramatic. But the medical seal of approval from Worcester's Dr Charles Hastings was more likely to have been the springboard from which John Corbett built and launched the chain of brine baths which, in time, treated between 200 and 300 patients a day.

'The Salt King', John Corbett has left his strong imprint in and around Droitwich. Stoke Grange, where he and Anna spent their first 20 years together, is now Avoncroft Museum. The beautiful chateau is now a hotel and restaurant. Strangely, in this monument to a lost love, the bridal suite and wedding-breakfast facilities are a speciality. Droitwich's remaining brine bath is fed from the salt spring, as is the lido – the only inland natural salt water pool in England.

A
Lament for
My Lady

THE 26th day of June 1920 was probably Great Witley's saddest day. The whole village united in mourning the loss of Rachel, wife of the 2nd Earl of Dudley, who had drowned while on holiday in Connemara, Ireland, in a bathing accident. What made it all so totally unexpected was that Lady Dudley, then about 50 years old, had been such an energetic, lively and even adventurous woman, capable of coping with most crises that came her way. And now the village had lost its 'First Lady' who, for 29 years, had been the pivot of village affairs. Though the inhabitants of Witley could not then have known it, a way of life which had prevailed for nearly three centuries under two rich and powerful families died with the Countess.

When, on the following day, the body of Countess Rachel was brought back to Witley Court, she was carried through silent rows of stunned employees. This was in sharp contrast to the day when many of them had been among the cheering lines of villagers forming the route along which the young Earl of Dudley brought his new bride. It had been such a wonderful day. Schoolchildren, the village band, 60 mounted tenants, a squadron of Worcestershire Yeomanry and householders at the doors of their gaily festooned cottages, had all combined to make this a red letter day in the history of Witley.

Some senior members of the staff had been present at the London society wedding of their master and Rachel Gurney, a Norfolk banker's daughter. Queen Victoria's heir, Prince Edward, had been an honoured guest, marking his friendship with the Dudley family and with this young Earl in particular. Glowing accounts of the splendid ceremony had been carried back to Witley and now the villagers could see for themselves the lovely girl the young Earl had married.

The celebrations to mark the young couple's homecoming lasted a week, commencing with a huge bonfire on Woodbury Hill, a firework display, dinner parties at the Court and generous hospitality to tenants, employees and their families all in turn. Then followed the busy, exciting years entertaining famous personalities, the Prince of Wales being a frequent visitor who enjoyed the sporting activities on the estate and lavish hospitality indoors. The indoor staff, particularly the housemaids, were entranced by the scenes in the beautiful, chandelier-lit drawing room. Local writer Dr R. O. Walker records them as lying prone on the floor of a landing, gazing through the banisters at the happy scene below, when a portly figure emerged from a bedroom behind them and stepped carefully between their prostrate forms with a smiling apology. It was the King (for he had then succeeded to the throne). Judging by the stories surrounding him in earlier days, one wonders whether his progress over them would have been quite so decorous in the past!

Those were exciting days, adding greatly to the prosperity of the Court staff, for there was plenty of work available and tips were generous. Even at that time, however, it appears that the children were brought up with an eye to careful spending – their favourite purchase at the village shop was Fry's twopenny chocolate cream bars, with the famous wrapper portraying the various stages of anticipation and delight upon the features of fortunate children.

But with all the lavish entertainment, Lady Rachel showed real concern for the under-privileged. In 1907 she accompanied the Earl on a voyage to the West Indies and was so troubled by conditions there on the sugar plantations that she returned to write a book, illustrated by Lord Dudley's photographs, describing it all with animation and sympathy. It was published by Constable under the title *Sunshine and Shadow in the West Indies*. Back at Witley she threw herself into the life of her own community with the same concern, while bringing up her own seven children. A new village school with modern plumbing and a home for needy girls were visible signs of her practical nature.

In the years just before the First World War, a German aviator named Gustave Hamel struck up an acquaintance with the Earl and became a frequent visitor, first alarming, then entrancing the villagers by his sudden appearances in his plane and descents from the sky. The adventurous Countess went up with Hamel on several occasions for an exciting spin.

The First World War brought new challenges. The Dudleys' heir, Lord Ednam, joined his father on active service and in their long absences it fell to the Countess's lot to keep the farmlands thriving, gather crops, settle landgirls to work and comfort the bereaved as one after another of the villagers fell in battle. Both the Earl and his son were wounded and invalided out. At the end of hostilities, it grieved the Earl that of his regiment only a few survived to attend his welcome home party.

In 1920 Lady Rachel went alone to Connemara for a holiday. No one at Witley was to see her again. She died in the green waters at Connemara and was brought back next day to be laid in the Garden of Rest which she herself had designed with loving care. Sixteen workmen of the estate were her bearers, and the grave was lined with rosemary, white lilac and honeysuckle.

It was said afterwards that the bell which tolled that day for My Lady tolled also for the passing of an era. Within three months the Witley people were dismayed to find the estate being divided up for sale in separate lots. The house and farm was bought by a Kidderminster carpet manufacturer who had risen from the designer's bench to own his own company.

Many old familiar landmarks were shut off from the public. The old splendour and largesse had gone for ever. It was almost an anti-climax when, in 1937, the beautiful house was gutted by fire and fell into the hands of demolition merchants.

Happily the beautiful and now famous Great Witley church was saved from the same fate by a change of wind on that night of disaster. Thousands of visitors each year come to admire its unique features and to gaze at the ruins of the lovely family home, once so vital a part of Witley in the capable hands of My Lady Rachel.

Coaching
Days

A VID readers of *The Pickwick Papers*, *Vanity Fair* and *Tom Brown's Schooldays* have probably cherished for years a romantic picture of coach travel. But it was not greatly appreciated by its early patrons. In 1663 one young boy wrote an account of his first journey:

'Honoured Father,
My journie was in noe ways pleasant, being forced to ride in the boote all the waye. Ye company up with mee were persons of great quality, knights and ladyes. My journie's expense was thirty shillings. This travail hath soe indisposed mee that I am resolved never to ride again in ye coach. I am extremely hott and feverish. What this may tend to I know not. I have not yet advised with any doctor.'

Hopefully the plaintive one got over his ordeal, for coaching as a means of public transport had come to stay.

Since the horses only averaged a speed of six miles an hour. journeys tended to stretch to two or three days, so the need for staying power was paramount. Certain rules had to be established, especially on steep gradients:

'First Class Passengers Inside – Keep Your Seats,
Second Class Passengers in Basket – Get Out And Walk,
Third Class Passengers On The Roof – Get Out And Push.'

Providing everybody toed the line all went well. It was quite useless to argue with the coachman. Once he took his place on the box, reins in hand, his word was law. Optimistic passengers cherished the hope that he was not in league with unscrupulous innkeepers en route where they would be forced to make unnecessary stops.

Worcester became an important stage on coaching journeys from north to south and great pride was exhibited when the distance from Liverpool was completed in eleven hours, despite the need to stop every twelve miles to change horses. The turnaround was completed with all the haste and excitement of a relay race. Competition between rival coaches was quite fierce by the 1830s. The *Birmingham Old Fly* and the *Berkeley Hunt* were frequently in Worcester where there were several good coaching inns, the Hop Pole and the Star and Garter seemingly the principal ones. The bustle and excitement surrounding their arrivals and departures attracted a good crowd of onlookers. Teams of horses were exchanged and passengers hurried in for a snatched meal with noisy demands for quick attention.

Even 200 years after coach travel became the norm for public transport, passengers were still fearful about their safety. It was not unknown for passengers to draw up their wills when purchasing their travel tickets! In the summer of 1836 Mrs Mary Bomford set out from Church Lench near Evesham to take a coach for the West Country on holiday. She had to report first to a coaching inn at Worcester and wrote immediately on arrival at her destination to her young husband:

'My very dear Joseph,
    We are just now settled here after a most fatiguing journey and I write by the first post because I know you will be anxious about us . . . The coach was very heavily loaded. We were delighted with the scenery. It was most romantic, large conical hills covered entirely with larches on one side of the road and rocks on the other. The road is

tolerably good but appears dangerous. We travelled many miles without any boundary whatever to the road on one side and the surface many yards below us so that if the coach were to upset it would be certain death. . .'

The Bomfords and fellow travellers must have been greatly comforted when, two years after that journey, a law was passed against 'furious driving'. After 1840 the penalty for speeding was a spell on the treadmill, which seems an admirable way of making the punishment fit the crime. Otherwise a driver, particularly after refreshment en route, could get literally carried away, terrified passengers being at his mercy.

The *Worcestershire Telegraph* left the Star and Garter Inn at Worcester at 3.30 every afternoon except Sunday, travelling through Pershore, Oxford and on to London – 'fast coaches at very reduced prices' according to the posters. From Worcester to London cost 28 shillings but outside travellers paid only 13 shillings. It was a calamitous day when the *Telegraph's* fore axle broke at the bottom of Hanwell Hill. The coach went over with a crash and all, including the driver were badly injured. Yet one intrepid soul, who had his collarbone broken, hurried off as soon as it was set, to find another coach and continue his journey!

In the last years of the 19th century Worcester city became noted as the home of the foremost carriage builders of the day. A coachbuilder named McNaught, who had distinguished himself by designing the prize chariot at the Great Exhibition, joined a local firm of coachbuilders and established carriage works and showrooms on a splendid, imposing site in the Tything, where now Kay's Mail Order offices are in occupation. So skilled was this firm that orders came in from many parts of the world as well as special orders for the Lord Mayor of London's coach and other state chariots. Those were prosperous and exciting days and it is sad that after a fire broke out, it caused such serious damage that the firm never recovered, despite the continued beauty and skill of its handiwork.

Happily Worcestershire does not seem to have suffered so

greatly from highwaymen as did other counties, but it is on record that the most notorious one of all, Dick Turpin, made a visit to Kempsey, a village some four miles west of the city. His victim is said to have been the 5th Earl of Coventry who, in 1739, was waylaid by means of a felled tree being laid across the road. Turpin emerged from the shadows with his usual salutation, and relieved the nobleman of his cash and watch, yet he responded to a plea to spare from his demands the miniature of a lovely lady. In return the Earl gave him, by way of a ransom, an order for 30 guineas to be recovered from his agent at Severn Stoke, some four to five miles further along the road. The whole transaction seems to have been conducted in gentlemanly fashion. The order was honoured by the Earl's agent, and the lady's honour, along with the miniature, was saved, no blood being shed.

Dr Johnson, in his *Lives of the Highwaymen* records a rather more entertaining encounter in the area with one John Over, son of a shoemaker, who stopped the Worcester stagecoach. It is said that many travellers carried firearms to protect themselves against robbery, but very few of them ever showed resistance when the time came. This was just such an occasion. When John Over demanded money and goods from the unfortunate victims, they complied. Then it came to the turn of an attractive lady passenger, and the highwayman fell instantly in love! Nevertheless, true to his calling, he relieved the lady of 20 guineas, but promised that if she would give him her address he intended only to borrow the sum and then return it to her. She complied with the request and quite soon afterwards received an audacious letter from the robber. It was she, declared John Over, who was the greater robber. He had taken but a few paltry guineas from her, but she had stolen his heart!

If the highwayman had returned her 20 guineas the lady might have been more impressed. As it was she replied:

'You have broken your word in not sending me what you villainously took from me . . . Let me tell you, lest you have too great a conceit of yourself, that you are the first to my recollection whom I have ever hated and, sealing my hatred with the hopes of quickly reading your dying speech, and in case you die in London, I presume to subscribe myself,

Yours, *never* to command . . .'

Whether there was a sequel to this tale we shall never know, but hopefully the shoemaker's wayward son was shamed into making reparation.

Coach travel held sway for more than 200 years before the railway enterpreneurs came along to expedite travel and perhaps offer greater safety. But what sad days they were when, one by one, the stage-coaches were withdrawn in the face of this competition. The coaching inns with their picturesque names lost the bustle and excitement of arrivals and expertly swift departures, and the clamour of hungry passengers around their dining tables. Overnight stops, of course, had engendered the human contact which makes life so much more interesting. The boot boy at the guest's door with spotless footwear, the ostler's call in the yard below, the clatter of horses' hooves from the stables, the waiter and the buxom maids answering the summons of countless bells, all in turn faded into memory. The innkeeper had to adapt to a different clientele or close up for ever when 'No more was heard the mellow winding horn waking the drowsy slumbers of the morn.'

Murder
in the
Clent Hills

ABOUT seven churches have been named after St Kenelm and though doubts have been expressed as to whether he really existed, a number of ancient chroniclers featured him in their records. The monk Florence of Worcester is quite positive about his tragic story. Writing well into the 11th century, 250 years after the drama, the monk relates the death of St Kenulf, King of Mercia, in AD 819 and says that he was the father of a daughter named Quendryth and a seven year old son, Kenelm, and that the boy succeeded his saintly father on the throne.

Quendryth was an ambitious young woman who resented her small brother's inheritance of power and prestige. She involved his guardian, or tutor, Ascebert, in a plot to assassinate him and perhaps the most astonishing thing about the collaborator's agreement is that he thought it a privilege to be rewarded by an offer of marriage from that heartless young woman. But history books are full of vulnerable men manipulated by beautiful schemers, and Ascebert was no exception. He lured young Kenelm to a lonely spot in Clent and struck off the boy's head, thrusting the body out of sight into a hidden grave.

It would appear that the boy victim became known as a saint in later years, not only because of his untimely death during the years of innocence, but because of the curious legends which became woven around the discovery of his body in a wooded thicket among the Clent Hills.

After Kenelm's death, wrote Florence the monk, 'From the child's pure milk-white head a milk-white dove soared to heaven on golden wings'. Mindful of the church's teaching that the soul rises from the body at the moment of death and passes into heaven, this is a reasonable interpretation and Florence seems content to close the tale on that reassuring note.

But others took the story further. William Caxton featured it in his *Golden Legend*. The white dove ascending to heaven was, he said, the bearer of the little boy's soul and he related a presentiment of this event which came to the boy in the form of 'a marvellous dream' one night. Kenelm saw a tree growing so high that it reached to the stars and became illumined with the brightness of burnished gold. Its branches were laden with blossom, fruit and bright lights. Then, still in the dream, his tutor (Caxton spells his name Askeberd) appeared on the scene and felled the tree to the ground with a crash, whereupon the dreamer, the young king, 'made for himself white wings, as of a dove, and flew up to heaven.'

Caxton goes on to relate a further occurrence following the death of the boy and the stealthy burial:

'A poor widow who had a white cow drove it to pasture in Clent wood daily; but the cow leaving the wood sought the valley where Kenelm was buried, and lay all day long by the king's grave without food, but when evening was come she returned home, and the milk she gave was twice as much as that of other cows. Wherefore the place was called Cowbage.'

This pastoral scene gives an odd slant to the story, yet there is something quite affecting about the picture of this patient creature keeping her day-long vigil beside the little grave. And it is not at all unbecoming that the animal guardian should be a cow, whose natural expression is one of gentle gravity.

The story continues with a white dove bearing a scroll into the presence of the Pope as he sang Mass at St Peter's in Rome. In letters of gold the inscription ran:

'In Clent, in Cowbage, Kenelme Kingborn,
Lyeth under a thorn, his hede of shorn'.

The understandable puzzlement of the Pope was relieved when an Englishman made a timely arrival on the scene and related Kenelm's story. The Pope then contacted Wylfryde, Archbishop of Canterbury, and a search was made of the hills. Aided by the widow's story, the body of the little king was found in its shallow grave.

The exhumation of the little king was not without incident. 'There welled up on that spot a fair spring which is called St Kenelm's Well to this day' and as the body was being borne away with all due solemnity a dispute arose between the men of Gloucester and the men of Worcester as to who should have possession of it for reburial.

It is said that Winchcombe Abbey, near Cheltenham, became the last resting place of the little king's bones, alongside those of his father. But St Kenelm's Chapel, on the northern slope of a valley between two Clent hills, is Worcestershire's tribute to the boy king, where he is well commemorated in richly coloured mosaic and other glass, and in the carved figure on the fine lychgate. An archway on the east wall is said to have once led to the nearby spring which was Nature's own tribute to him, on the very spot where the white cow kept her vigil.

The Dreamer
and the
Rocking Throne

IN June 1887, in the twilight of a long, exciting day, a sturdy fair-haired youth strode across a Worcestershire common, gazing with eager anticipation toward the distant summit of Malvern's highest hill. Within moments a flare of light sprang to view, pierced the descending shadows, and beamed a signal across the county. Seconds later, in quick succession, other beacons sprang to light on the lower summits of Ankerdine, Berrow, Woodbury, Abberley and the Clee Hills. They formed a distant arc of flaring torchlight around the watching figure. It was a moment which the 19 year old student was never to forget. It stirred in him a corresponding flame, deepening to ecstasy the pride and joy of his love for England, and for his Worcestershire home in particular. This was the climax of the Golden Jubilee Day of Queen Victoria.

On that splendid night of pageantry it would not have crossed the minds of any man or woman in England (least of all that of the Bewdley-born youth himself) that 50 years hence the throne which now seemed so secure would be rocked by scandal, dissention and indecision. Even more unlikely would it have seemed that this very ordinary, pleasant young man would be the one to reach out a steadying hand at a time of grave crisis and who would, in the opinion of many, save the British monarchy. His name was Stanley Baldwin.

THE DREAMER AND THE ROCKING THRONE

In the year following the Jubilee, Alfred Baldwin, a successful ironfounder whose works were at Wilden, near Stourport, summoned his son from Cambridge to join him in the family business. It was not the career which young Stanley would have chosen. He had more in common with his mother's family from nearby Ribbesford, who were lovers of literature, and were painters and poets of some distinction. He shared the patriotism and love of language of his cousin Rudyard Kipling. He would have loved to have expressed himself on easel and canvas, as did the uncles who sometimes took him to Europe on exciting visits. But he was an only child and he was also the heir to whom his father looked for partnership. He could not fail him.

But duty and discipline, balancing the books, and inspiring loyalty while giving leadership and understanding to working men, was to prepare him for a wider sphere of influence than Harrow or Cambridge had ever done. The forge at Wilden proved a splendid school for democracy and provided the common touch. When his father secured a seat at Westminster as Member for West Worcestershire, 25 year old Stanley became Works Gaffer. It was a job which called for more than a stopwatch and a slide rule over the next 15 years.

Stanley Baldwin had a sincere, open expression which invited trust and confidences. He was the typical country squire, enjoying a little farming and pig breeding. He was a man of simple tastes who revelled in the simplicity of the Worcestershire people around him.

Loving the life of the countryside, Stanley Baldwin might well have been content to serve its rural interests alone, but on the death of his father in 1908 the Bewdley folk elected him to represent them in the House of Commons. Thus, for the best part of 30 years, wider duties and heavier responsibilities took him away from his beloved county and his home in the village of Astley.

'Who is he?' enquired someone when the bluff, farmer type with the cherrywood pipe began to emerge as a personality in

Parliament, 'All we know of him is that he comes from Worcestershire.'

'And all we know of Worcestershire,' responded Winston Churchill, 'is that it makes sauce!'

In the years that followed, Mr Baldwin's progress astonished even his own Conservative party, which he led for 14 years, three times as Prime Minister. His record of honest dealings, sound commonsense and respect for the working man seem to be unquestioned. His accomplishments, challenges, dilemmas and defeats are recorded in history. He had to cope with the General Strike of 1926 and ten years later the 'plain man's Prime Minister', as Sir Arthur Bryant calls him, was faced with a crisis of a contrasting nature.

In 1936, though most of England was unaware of it, their Prime Minister carried the burden of the knowledge that the new King, Edward VIII, had formed a liaison with the American divorcee, Mrs Wallis Simpson. When it became obvious that the King had no intention of relinquishing the association, Mr Baldwin took himself unhappily to the Palace and tried to reason with the King and persuade him to uphold the principles on which the monarchy had rested for so many years. The Prime Minister had a genuine liking for King Edward, and the King had formed a good relationship with Mr Baldwin during a tour of Canada earlier. But many hours of consultation, 'wrestling with the King's conscience', as he put it later, was of no avail. 'He is the only man I have talked with', commented the Prime Minister wearily, 'that seems to have no spiritual ground on which to appeal. His mind was made up and those who know His Majesty know what that means.'

So on Mr Baldwin's shoulders fell the responsibility, author-ised of course by the Cabinet, of rejecting all compromises and facing the 41 year old King with an ultimatum, the choice between the throne and the marriage, with results that are known the world over. For one grim day there came a thinly veiled threat that the King might overturn protocol and appeal to the public to support him, fracturing the firm basis of the relationship between Parliament and the English throne. But somehow the crisis was averted, and it may well be Mr Baldwin's demeanour which inclined the King to make his choice with dignity, for as he turned away from the King at that point the Prime Minister commented sadly 'Then I hope you may find happiness where you believe it is to be found.' After leaving England the ex-King said later 'The Prime Minister is the only man who said a kind word to me about the future.'

The abdication and the ushering in of the splendid era of rule by the King's brother and his well loved family brought Mr Balwin's career to a close. Worcestershire welcomed him back to the sounds and sights that he loved. The ex-Prime Minister was heard to comment 'When I was a little boy in Worcestershire, reading history books, I never thought I should have to interfere between a King and his mistress.'

The
Music
Makers

A September day in 1905 brought an emotionally charged moment into the life of William Elgar, retired piano tuner and ex-proprietor of a music shop in Worcester's High Street. He was seated at an open window above those premises, looking down upon a dignified procession winding its way between the Guildhall and the Cathedral. The old man's third son, Sir Edward Elgar, was being granted the Freedom of the City. Surrounded today by a group of civic dignitaries, he was clad in the robes of Yale, the most recent university to award the honorary degree of Doctor of Music to the greatest composer of his time.

As the procession drew level with the old man's window there was a momentary pause. The son raised his cap, looked up at his father and saluted him. A second later the cavalcade was on its way and as the eyes of the old man followed it he would have noted with added pleasure that the man in mayoral regalia presiding over this event was none other than his son's boyhood friend, Hubert Leicester.

The procession passed from sight. The crowds melted away, and the new Freeman's father was left to his pride and his memories.

William had been a mere 19 year old when his London employers sent him to Witley Court to tune the pianofortes of the widowed Queen Adelaide. She was spending her last years under the roof of the 1st Earl of Dudley. This had led to other appointments in Worcestershire and ultimately to the Soho music firm losing their employee. Basing himself at the Greenings' coffee shop in Worcester, he located premises to form a base for his piano tuning, and in which to start a music shop. His acquaintance with Anne Greening ripened into love. They married in 1848, the same year in which he was made organist of St George's Catholic church.

His touch on both piano and organ has been described as 'beautiful', and attracted crowds to the church where he was to play for 37 years – though it is said that he himself impiously slipped off to the nearby Hop Market Hotel during the sermon!

The Elgars' first three children were born presumably 'over the shop' and were brought up in the Catholic faith as well as in the music-loving atmosphere surrounding their father. It was a busy household but Mrs Elgar managed to be at the shop counter while her husband travelled the countryside on his thoroughbred horse to reach his clients and to 'tune with love' their instruments wherever he went. As the family grew, the Elgars moved to a village three miles to the west of the city, to the cottage at Broadheath which has now become famous as the birthplace of their third son, Edward.

A little later the family moved back into the city to live over the shop, which was then at No 1 Edgar Street, in close proximity to the cathedral, with which their business had established close links. When he was 9 or 10 years old, Edward was found one day with pencil and a scrap of manuscript paper trying to interpret in music the sound which he described as 'the reeds singing' on the river bank. Nobody appears to have been impressed by it, but for Edward himself it was a lasting experience. Many years later he was to write in a letter to a friend:

'I am still at heart the dreamy child who used to be found in the reeds by Severn side with a sheet of paper trying to fix the sounds and longing for something very great – source, texture and all else unknown. I am still looking for this – in strange company sometimes – but as a child and as a young man no single person was ever kind to me.'

It must be that the writer was in one of his occasional bouts of depression at the time of writing. He could be very sensitive and was prone to discouragement. Perhaps his first childish efforts on the violin had not met with acclaim – he had only about six months tuition all told. Be that as it may, he was extremely fortunate in finding a splendid boyhood friend in Hubert Leicester, whose home was nearby. When they were eleven years old both boys were enrolled at Littleton House School, at so modest a fee that the future composer was able to claim later that his total private education cost no more than £37, plus a few pounds more spent on elementary violin lessons and a little brief tuition on the pianoforte under local teachers.

By the time they were 15 the boys had finished their schooling and were consigned to office stools in the dry and dusty atmosphere of lawyers' offices. Edward Elgar badly wanted to go to Leipzig to study music under German masters, but it seems his father could not find the money. But at least he rescued Edward from those uncongenial surroundings within a year and took him into the family business, with its gleaming instruments and racks of exciting music.

An appointment as his father's assistant organist at the Catholic church drew father and son closer, and there was probably no greater pleasure than shared evenings at the Crown Hotel with the Worcester Glee Club. Tankards of ale and lighted tapers before them at long tables, club members puffed in contentment at churchwarden pipes, planning programmes. Soon the son outstripped his father as a violinist and in 1879 22 year old Edward became the club's conductor and had a number of pianoforte pupils of his own.

The music shop must have missed Edward for a while when he managed to scrape together a little money to go to London for violin lessons from Adolphe Pollitzer. He made splendid progress but near-starvation forced his return to Worcester, to make the best of whatever local opportunities came his way. He became acquainted with choral masterpieces through the Three Choirs Festivals and by 1881 was playing first violin in the orchestra. Hubert Leicester's friendship was still a joy and when Hubert became choir master at the Catholic church he was closely involved with both Elgars, father and son.

So the years fled by. William Elgar must have been a happy man surrounded by his talented family but he would have known all along that Edward felt unfulfilled, that he pined to break free from business and from teaching restraints, to study under great masters and to give his mind to composition. He would have seen Edward's struggle for development and recognition, and could not have been unaware of the touch of bitterness in Edward when delays and disappointments attended his work.

But the tide turned when Edward met and married Caroline Alice Roberts in 1889. He was then 32, and she had reached the age of 40. Her belief and delight in her husband's talent was unbounded. Though she had herself enjoyed some literary success in earlier years, she put aside everything to give Edward the opportunities which had eluded him for so long.

It was ten years before Mrs Elgar's confidence in her husband's genius was justified by public acclaim and many accounts have been written by professional critics about the composer's accomplishments in the years thereafter. Though he became world famous Edward Elgar's name will for ever by linked with the Worcestershire countryside, to which he attributed a considerable measure of his inspiration. He was generous also in acknowledging his indebtedness to his mother, Anne Elgar, to her romantic and poetic mind and her love of nature and good books, all of which she lovingly shared with her children. Visiting Edward's home in Storridge, near Malvern, on one occasion Edward's mother gazed toward a distant peak and entreated him to capture something of the past history lingering there and to present it to the world in words and music.

His response came in the form of the cantata *Caractacus*, telling the legend of that ancient King of Britain making his last heroic stand from a camp in the Malvern Hills. The words were by H. A. Acworth, but Elgar requested a final note of patriotism and it ends by highlighting the Romans' admiration for their captive's courage and with a prediction that the Roman Empire would fall and Britain should rise again!

It was not perhaps Elgar's finest work. That would come two years later with *The Dream of Gerontius* winning worldwide acclaim in 1900. But hopefully Anne Elgar derived great pleasure from sharing with her illustrious son that perceptive awareness of drama and beauty in the Worcestershire countryside.

By 1905 honours were flowing in from academies, colleges and universities on both sides of the Atlantic and in Europe, culminating in his knighthood. Even so, it may well be that the granting of the Freedom of the City of Worcester on that September day was as delightful an occasion for Sir Edward Elgar as it was for the old man at the High Street window.

The Spy
With the Fiddle

IT seems incredible that the nailmaking industry of the 17th century should owe its success to a Worcestershire lad who sallied forth to Scandinavia with nothing more in hand than his beloved fiddle. The story may, as some assert, be just a legend, but it crops up in various journals and with slightly differing details that somehow combine to give the basic story the ring of truth. The tale is worth retelling.

It was Richard Foley who made the journey in 1600, as a wandering minstrel, to the Ural mountains and then on to the Swedish mines near Upsala. Here his music had charms enough to win the confidence and friendship of a local miller, who had evolved a process of making nails out of blocks of metal by the use of circular cutting plates. The metal was easily slit into appropriate sizes and shape and the miller was on the way to making a fortune for himself. He had found markets throughout Europe, which threatened the future of English nailmakers who still had to rely on more primitive methods of production. Forges in North Worcestershire were having to heat bars of metal to high temperatures, then roll them into broad sheets so they could be laboriously cut, with nothing more powerful than hand chisels, into nail-shaped widths and lengths.

All of this would have gone over the head of any normal, music-loving minstrel with nothing but his art to occupy his skills and delight his companions. But Richard Foley was not bent solely on harmony and song, nor had he come to Scandinavia to admire the scenery, grand though it was compared to his native Dudley. Back in North Worcestershire, as Richard was well aware, a seemingly infinite supply of mineral resources had become available to feed the furnaces and forges of hardworking, enterprising manufacturers. Richard himself had started his working life as a salesman for the rough-cut nails of the day, later being promoted to work as a forge-master. His ambition grew with his responsibilities, but he became convinced that the greater success of the Continental and Swedish nail manufacturers who were cornering the overseas markets, was due to some method or component against which the English workers, despite their sweat and toil for a mere pittance, could not compete. So he took up his fiddle and took ship across the North Sea.

Even when he arrived back in Worcestershire with his new knowledge, the battle was not yet won. Richard found a sponsor who was impressed by his eager tale, but he must have been frustrated to find his efforts less successful than forecast. It speaks for his sense of dedication to the task, though not perhaps for his morality in method, in that he did not give up. Returning to his unsuspecting hosts in Sweden with his fiddle and his disarming tunes, he gained entry into the mill again. This time he got permission to spend the night on the premises and took the opportunity to scan documentation and diagrams which were on hand. Building on the knowledge already gained, he returned home more confident of future success. His confidence was not misplaced. He established furnaces and forges at Stourbridge, Kinver and Caunsall, and the beginnings of a considerable fortune for himself and his heirs.

Richard settled in Stourbridge and Worcestershire became the centre of England's nailmaking industry, expanding into other areas of ironmongery in the first years of the 17th century. It was the beginning of a long and impressive association between the Foleys and Worcestershire. The first home of the founding family in Stourbridge was on the spot on which the Talbot Hotel now stands, but in later years the Foleys moved to much more impressive surroundings.

Success seems to have softened Richard to some extent. He was a hard man in business, and nailmaking was a hard way for the men under him to make a living. Some worked in their own cottages and sheds, whole families toiling a 12 hour day for a few shillings a week. Yet Richard Foley began to share his wealth in charitable endowments around the area. His business was continued by his son Thomas, with growing success. His grandson Robert became High Sheriff of Worcestershire and the owner occupier of Kenswick Manor, before establishing the family seat at Witley Court.

For more than 200 years the family exercised an influence for good in the county and their name abounds in street names and park lands over a 30 mile radius. That such success was built up by a nail salesman with musical fingers is perhaps less surprising than that he did it with such humble, unimpressive merchandise. But, of course, like every successful entrepreneur Richard Foley made his fortune by recognising the true value of what he had to offer in relation to the needs of his day. He would have agreed with his namesake of 1758 – in *Poor Richard's Almanac*:

> For the want of a nail, the shoe was lost;
> For the want of a shoe, the horse was lost;
> For the want of a horse, the rider was lost!

When Samuel Pepys the diarist dined with Richard's grandson, Thomas, in 1664, he recorded for posterity:

> 'We were entertained by Mr Foley, the ironmonger, with a good plain dinner but I expected music, the missing of which spoiled my dinner though there was the consolation of a very good discourse.'

Sadly it would seem that the family did not inherit Richard's musical talent!

73

Murder
Most Foul

IT is doubtful whether the village of Upton Snodsbury,
through which the Worcester–Alcester road threads its
way, has ever been more divided than it was over John
Palmer, when he stood trial for double murder at Worcester
Assizes on 1st April, 1708. The tragic victims in the case were
none other than his own mother and her serving maid, whose
home was half a mile away from John Palmer's own.

On the night of 7th November 1707, smoke and flames were
seen to be shooting up into the darkness from the windows
and roof of old Mrs Palmer's house at Town End. A plucky
neighbour of Mrs Palmer's, first on the scene, made a bold
dash into the house through choking smoke and made straight
for the downstairs room in which he knew her to sleep. There
seemed to be two figures on the bed. He grasped the clothing
of the nearest one and stumbled away, only to drop his burden
on the threshold. By now other hands were reaching out to
help him and the still body of Mrs Palmer was hoisted into the
garden. The neighbour turned back for the second woman,
but in vain. He staggered back only just in time to avoid the
crash of burning timbers as the roof fell in and set light to
everything on the ground floor. Breathless, he joined the
growing crowd in the garden and found them recoiling in
shock. By the light of the shooting flames, bloodstains on their
lifeless neighbour's face and neck, together with marks of a
lethal injury upon her head, revealed that this was no accident.

As constables and firemen converged upon the spot, a villager sped to the victim's son at nearby Libery to break the news. When he arrived all was dark and silent until his frantic knocking upon the door brought John Palmer, in night attire, to an upper window which was thrust open in haste as the owner leaned over the sill. 'Bad news, Mr Palmer,' gasped the man in the garden below, 'Your mother's dead and her house is afire!' 'God forbid!' breathed the man at the window, 'I – I'll be down . . . wait a minute. Wait there!'

The two men sped off in the direction of Town End, where it seemed that half the villagers of Upton Snodsbury had congregated in the roadway facing what had been Alice Palmer's front door. All moved aside to let the two men through to the still blazing embers, and the group around Mrs Palmer's body noted with awe that her son could not face the ordeal of bending over her. Shocked and agitated, he nodded dumbly when it was proposed that his mother's body should be brought to rest at his house, the home she had shared with him some years earlier.

Enquiries began at daybreak but it was nearly a week before a clue to the murder emerged. Certain articles, thought to have been consumed in the fire, were discovered in a cottage in the village by a mystified housewife. The bundle consisted of some linen sheets, a pewter plate and some table napkins marked with the initials AP. It transpired that it had been brought there by the cottager's brother, a man named Giles Hunt who was soon apprehended and lodged in the gaol at Worcester Castle. Hunt was a fairly simple man and terrified at his situation. He soon admitted his complicity in the Town End fire, and named a Tom Dun as his associate. Some delay ensued in picking up Dun because he was also known as William Hobbins, but under that name he was subsequently charged with involvement in the murder of Mrs Palmer and Hester Loxley, the maid.

Giles Hunt yielded to the temptation to turn informer and the name of Thomas Symonds cropped up. From then on the net began to close in. Symonds was known to frequent bars and inns throughout the district. He came of a good family with County connections, but had been seen in strange company more than once. The authorities were not at all satisfied with his stout denials of all knowledge of the Town End affair.

It was also known from Hunt's confession, for such it amounted to, that a fourth man had been involved, a shadowy figure whose name Hunt never heard. Indeed the very thought of him seemed to terrify the informer. He dared not say more, he cried 'or the Devil would tear me in pieces!' They had met in darkness and later he had glimpsed him briefly by candle-light. With great difficulty a brief description was got from him – a slim person, dark hair 'or a natural perigwig', pale faced, quite well dressed. Within hours John Palmer was brought to the gaol at Worcester Castle.

The trial opened at the end of March 1708. All except Giles Hunt pleaded Not Guilty and defended themselves vigorously. But Hunt, chief witness for the prosecution, had a long and chilling tale to tell. Promise of a pardon had loosened his tongue, fear of the Devil notwithstanding!

Hunt had been approached by William Hobbins at Pershore Fair and invited to join him in 'a bold attempt upon a house at Town End' where two women lived alone. He was bidden to meet Hobbins again on the following Thursday under the yew tree on the Spetchley road, and was to keep utter silence until then. When Hunt arrived on the night of 7th November the appointed spot was silent. He waited for what seemed a long time and grew very nervous under the thick, overhanging boughs of the tree, as well he might, if only because yew trees have a centuries-long association with graveyards in that locality. Hunt had begun to edge nervously away when he was stopped by a low call from behind a nearby hedge. It was Hobbins, who now joined him and led him on along the Spetchley road in the direction of Upton Snodsbury where, he said, they were to meet 'two others engaged in the matter'.

They arrived and waited behind the huge tree trunk of the Churchill Oak. Two figures shortly emerged from the opposite direction. Hobbins greeted one of them as Symonds but the fourth man at first remained silent. Then he demanded, in a sharp, nervous tone, whether Hobbins's crony was to be trusted. Hobbins vouched for Hunt in confident tones, but the slim questioner was not satisfied. He made Giles Hunt kneel on the root-gnarled ground beneath the oak and swear that if he ever disclosed the matter they were going upon, 'the Devil would tear him from limb to limb and that the next bite he should eat should be his damnation.' In no little trepidation Hunt complied, word for word and all four then set out for Town End.

In the road outside Mrs Palmer's house the fourth man drew back, urging the rest on without him, but Symonds exclaimed 'It is your business and if you don't, no one goes.' To this the man replied after another pause, 'Let's go on! Damn her – I never loved her!' The speaker then sat on the front doorstep, motioning the others around to the back door where Hunt arrived first and noticed a brass kettle on the step.

Although it was past midnight a faint glow shone from a nearby window. Peering in, Hunt saw an elderly woman sitting by the fireside while another person was warming the bed in readiness for the night. Symonds, who seemed to be in charge of the operation, stepped up to the back door stealthily, but was surprised by it swinging inwards and the old lady appearing on the threshold – as if, Hunt conjectured afterwards, she had come to pick up the brass kettle.

Symonds and Hobbins rushed forward and propelled Mrs Palmer backwards into the building, and as she fell one of them struck her with the butt end of a crew-barrelled pistol. With a shriek she collapsed on the floor and the second attacker stabbed at her several times with a short-bladed weapon. By this time Hester Loxley had come running in response to her mistress's cry. Sadly she suffered the same fate and fell across the body of Mrs Palmer.

Symonds then rushed to the front door and admitted the fourth man, who stooped swiftly over the body of Mrs Palmer, twisted her skirt until he could plunge his hand into a large pocket, and withdrew a bunch of keys. From a chest at the foot of the bed he brought out two sheets of parchment with seals dangling, a small box and a bag of money which, when opened and shared in varying amounts, contained about £40. The two still forms were laid on the bed and some effort was made to set fire to it. This was abandoned when one of the ringleaders went up and set the roof thatch alight. The four guilty men then fled the house and separated.

The witness was asked to identify the fourth man whose name was not known to him. He claimed that he recognised Palmer as the man he had seen only by flickering candle-light inside the house on that fatal night.

Palmer's trial, following on immediately after that of Hobbins and Symonds, opened on 1st April. Pleading that so unreliable a witness as Hunt could not be taken seriously, as he had been bribed by the offer of a pardon, Palmer's counsel called character witnesses who spoke well of him. But when the prosecution called theirs, a contrasting picture emerged. A former servant of Mrs Palmer revealed that the son had frequently borrowed money from his mother, who had been made unwelcome when living under his roof.

It was probably the weaver whose evidence swayed the jury finally. His seasonal visit had occurred only 24 hours before Mrs Palmer's death. She paid him for flax and commented that only the day before she had completed spinning the previous season's supply. She welcomed the weaver's company, pressing him to stay until nearly midnight because her son had taken her guard dog away recently and she was troubled that it had not been returned to her. She rarely went to bed before midnight, she told him, as she was nervous and this shortened the night watches. She confided in him also that her son had borrowed money and that it angered him if she sought its return or requested interest.

The jury took only two hours to bring in the same verdict as for Hobbins and Symonds. All three were sentenced to death, together with a John Allen who (with Giles Hunt and Thomas

Symonds) had committed an earlier similar crime at nearby Bradforton. The informer Hunt, though guilty of both evil crimes, got his pardon.

The comdemned men persisted in stubborn denials of guilt. In the time remaining to them, the Bishop of Oxford (who was also Dean of Worcester) entreated them all to make a confession of guilt in order to clear their consciences and be better prepared to meet their Maker. The Bishop was clearly a genuine and persuasive man. He appears to have won the confidence of John Palmer, who indicated that he and his brother-in-law Symonds might yield. Overjoyed, the Bishop gained a three weeks respite for the two and got a brief, rather vague admission from each.

The two labourers went to the scaffold, but not before a bizarre farewell meeting was set up (by the good offices of the Bishop) with their two co-defendants. On their last fateful walk Allen and Hobbins were brought to a landing at the foot of a staircase, while the two 'gents' stood on a stairwell above them. Prompted by the Bishop, John Palmer cried out 'Hobbins, I have owned myself guilty and I advise you to do the same!', while Symonds similarly addressed the other man. It must have been something of an anti-climax when their partners in crime, looking up at the men on the stairwell, rejected in no uncertain terms the pious advice of the men who had landed them in their present predicament. Perhaps it was as well (Palmer and Symonds had been promised this) that they already had their hands bound in readiness for their next appointment! Sightseers were already assembled when the two went their way, unshriven, much to the good Bishop Talbot's disappointment.

Of Symonds' guilt, of course, there was little doubt. So when the time came for the second execution date it may have been no more than fitting, given the custom of those times, that his body joined those of the two on the gibbets which swayed in the breeze at the scene of their crimes.

But was John Palmer guilty of this horrible crime? He had an alibi for that night, and he gained little from his mother's death. We shall never know. Bishop Talbot tried to the end to get a clear confession from Palmer, but can have gained only slight comfort when Palmer's last words on the scaffold ended by asking 'God's mercies upon my "failings"'. As confessions go, it was something of a compromise. Even so, the good Bishop, into whose hands Palmer's forfeited estate was given by law after the execution, used the money to found and endow two excellent schools in the locality for the education and moral upbringing of 20 poor boys and ten poor girls. It was a memorial, of sorts. Moreover Bishop Talbot took under his own roof Palmer's infant son whom he raised and educated to honest manhood.

It was his final touch of grace upon Upton Snodsbury's grim tragedy.

Sports and Frolics

T IME appears to have stood still in the village of Throck-
morton even more than in other rural areas. Even now
the village church, part of which dates back to the 13th
century, has no mains power connected, and the worshippers
approach it from the roadway by means of a field track and
over a cattle grid. The field which then has to be crossed to
reach the church provides an ideal spot for the annual fete,
and one year it became a splendid setting for an entrancing
glimpse of old village life. The 20th century was banished
from the fete in front of the old grey church and the clock was
turned back 300 years. Everyone wore 17th century costume.

The Holbourne Consort Recorder Group contributed music
of the period, and Punch and Judy provided the usual 'audi-
ence participation'. Punch has been a favourite in England for
many generations, though of Italian origin. His original opening line was:

> 'I'm that little fellow
> Call'd Punchinello,
> Much beauty I carry about me;
> I'm witty and pretty,
> And come to delight ye;
> You cannot be merry without me!'

And for some reason, it is true that no Worcestershire event is complete without him, audacious though his other claims may be.

Soon skipping and Orange & Lemon teams swung into action, while customers clustered around the busy Spinning Wheel and well stocked stalls of preserves and pickles concocted from old recipes. Clay pipes, two-handled loving cups, beakers, curiously shaped jugs and other pottery of 17th century design were specially produced from a nearby 'village industry' ceramics firm. Appropriate refreshments, and perhaps the home-made wines and punchbowl, would have added to the high spirits with which to tackle games and contests on the Gannow (an old word for the playing field).

For villagers of bygone days costly toys were out of the question, but any handy fellow could whittle the sticks for ninepins, tipcat, whip-and-top, skittles, bowling hoops, shuffleboard, wooden dolls and the like. A very special attraction was Nine Men's Morris. A Morris Board, with holes bored in a geometrical design, was laid upon the turf and the nine 'men' – wooden 'pins' with a base broader than their tops – were made to stand, each in its marked hole. Crescent-shaped wooden pegs provided the ammunition with which to bombard the standing men, and the player's score was recorded as the 'uprights' fell.

'Cob' was a marbles contest, more easily set out because competitors simply aimed the marbles at a hole poked in the ground (golfing fashion), and woe betide the 'smiffter' who dared to apprehend and run off with the marbles! 'Bumb ball' was a kind of rounders, 'Cat Gallows' (alternatively called 'Jump Jack') required two upright poles (jumping stocks) over which to lay a crosspiece for gymnasts. 'Quack' was for boys and girls who could find a large pebble (called their quack). Each contestant lodged his quack upon a larger stone called a 'mother' and the challenge lay in pelting the pebble atop the mother until it was dislodged. The winner of each round then challenged the others.

Stones and pebbles, so freely available, provided ammunition for many a game even into the 20th century. 'Five Stones' could be picked up in any school playground. It is one of the oldest games in existence. Originally, in rural Worcestershire, it was played with the knuckle bones of sheep. Later, in more built up areas, pieces of clay and pebbles lying around sufficed. There are several variations of the game and skilled players devise a programme playing them in rotation to secure a champion. The basic skill is merely to catch as many of the five falling pebbles on the back of the hand as possible. He who fails to catch any at all is immediately 'out' and survivors go on to more skilful manoeuvres. The ultimate challenge is to lay four pebbles on the ground, toss up the fifth one, and snatch up the four before the one in the air descends on to the back of the hand.

Presumably the poorer folk had to find fun out of doors, and lively youngsters would have devised games later developed for the sports field.

For instance, one may safely conclude that 'Bandy' was probably the origin of hockey. Players armed themselves with sticks curved at the bottom end, with which to strike out at a 'cat', a small well-shaped piece of wood. Tennis and 'closhes' (probably a form of croquet) date back to the Middle Ages. France had a woman tennis champion named Mlle Angot as far back as 1426, but in England the king (Edward IV) sternly forbade both games in case they discouraged archery practice! 'Scoperils' is a very ancient game about which little detail is recorded. It was played with a kind of teetotum – a spinning toy made out of buttons – and is almost certainly pre-Elizabethan. The better known quoits comes down from the discus-throwing days of the Greeks and Romans.

The Maypole and Morris Dancers have been very much a part of Worcestershire life for many years. The gay ribbons, bedecked hats, stockinged legs, coloured kerchiefs and short sticks with which to smartly 'clack' against each other as the wearers leap and dance in formation, provide a colourful entertainment still on special occasions. In the Pershore area they travel around at Yuletide, like carol singers, usually with a 'tomfool', a clowning character with painted face. At one time dancing on the green was quite a common sight. That adults, after a hard day's work in the fields or at the forge, could so disport themselves, is a tribute to Worcestershire stamina!

Mops and hiring fairs, though events long past, must have provided a more lively setting for a Labour Exchange than today's sober establishments, but for men and women in need of work, no doubt it was not all fun and pleasure. Harvest Home however was not only the time for a farmer to provide a substantial meal in a large barn, but also an opportunity for unlimited drink and merriment. Not everyone regretted its passing!

Human nature being what it is, disconcerting tricks played upon unsuspecting victims have always been a source of fun, raising much merriment at the discomfiture of the unfortunate one. 'Catching an owl' was a countryside trick by which a man was lured to a barn by one confederate, and told he was to catch an owl by holding a sieve over his head while his companion shone the light of a lantern on it. This, he was promised, would attract the owl into the sieve. But a third man would be hiding in the loft overhead, and when the light shone on the sieve, the hidden conspirator above would merrily pour a pail of water into it! Perhaps a little less aggravating to its victims was the children's custom of tying together the doorhandles of adjoining houses, giving a smart rat-tat upon each door, then flying off to hide at some convenient corner, around which they could peep and enjoy the predicament of the neighbours answering the knocks upon their respective doors.

'Sheep, Sheep, Come Over' was a playground game, for it could not safely be conducted in a roadway when the motorcar began to appear on Worcestershire roads. Two rows of children faced each other (they were the sheep) with an 'outcast' in the centre, between the rows. At the given signal – a challenge from the other side – the sheep were obliged to fly smartly to the opposite 'goal' while the 'pig in the middle' tried to grab one of them as they hurtled past (no mean feat for a stationary figure). The captive, of course, had to take the place in the centre.

The noble sport of cricket was played centuries ago by the monks of Evesham. How did they run with those enveloping habits? The now celebrated Worcestershire team owes its inception to a committee composed mainly of clergymen from around the county and to the 4th Lord Lyttelton of Hagley Hall. They acquired the beautiful site alongside the river Severn with the great cathedral as its backdrop. It is said to be the loveliest pitch in England.

The first fixture was with Yorkshire in 1899. It was familiarly dubbed 'Worcestershire Sauce' versus 'Yorkshire Relish'. Worcestershire lost!

The Bartered Bride

BECAUSE the long, winding course of the river Severn formed the recognised boundary between England and Wales, Worcester was for centuries the chief border city. Its west side was actually in Welsh territory, on the opposite river bank to the main buildings. Worcester therefore became the obvious parleying point during the Middle Ages for the Welsh and their English rulers at such times as the latter made their royal progresses into the city. Such visits were not infrequent, for the citizens were known to be loyal and supportive to the Crown, and the city provided an attractive venue.

Despite the failure of the charismatic Llewellyn the Great to win any concessions for Wales from his brother-in-law, Henry III, in Worcester in 1224, Llewellyn, Prince of Cambria, some 50 years later, believed he could do better. As he grew to manhood, he won support from his countrymen, and people flocked to his standard. At last the whole of Cambria, right up to the hills which rose above the Severn, came under his rule. Lesser princes pledged their loyalty and he was acclaimed as Pendragon, their undoubted lord, who would win freedom.

So Llewellyn watched intently for the opportunity of a showdown with the English. It came on the eve of St Edward's Day in 1278 when Edward I rode into Worcester and took up his lodgings inside the city wall.

Prudently, Llewellyn obtained a parole enabling him to approach the castle openly. He also took the precaution of despatching his affianced bride Elianora (daughter of Simon de Montfort, Earl of Leicester) out into the Bristol Channel, there to embark on a short coastal voyage to a place of safety further north – just in case the English king's mood was not as receptive as the Welsh prince hoped!

Llewellyn reckoned without the foresight of the English. Elianora had scarcely settled in the outgoing vessel when an English ship was sighted, followed by a second pursuer, also English. Elianora was swiftly captured and was conveyed to Worcester even before her gallant young lover had arrived there with his precious parole in hand. His consternation on being acquainted with the news of his lady's capture can be imagined. His bargaining power had sadly diminished.

Llewellyn was offered an olive branch, none the less – a choice of a kind. His parole would be honoured. He could return to his supporters and never see Elianora again, or alternatively he must give up all claim to Wales apart from a small, limited area of wild and barren territory among the mountains, which he could hold as vassal to the English king.

Faced with this terrible dilemma Llewellyn surrendered at a ceremony inside the Chapter House, kissed the hand of King Edward, and had his betrothed restored to him. He and Elianora were married next day, surrounded by the wedding 'guests' who had defeated him. As for the honeymoon – he was promptly banished to the foot of Snowdon!

His reception in Wales was not a happy one. The warring Welsh accused Llewellyn ap Griffith of betraying his country for his lady-love. It is not true that 'all the world loves a lover' – the star had fallen in disgrace.

And he was not, alas, to live happily ever after. The marriage was destined to be tragically short. The hapless little bride died young and childless. But with her Llewellyn buried also his parole and his truce. He rallied his forces again, and it is a tribute to his charisma and to their dogged faith in the Welsh cause, that his followers rose to rally to his banner.

The Welsh plunged once again into battle along the banks of the Severn. It would be good to relate a happy ending, but it was not to be. Llewellyn fought valiantly but fell in the field. One of the foe struck off his head and it was borne away in triumph to the Tower of London, to be spiked aloft on display.

An aged crone had once foretold that one day Llewellyn would wear a crown in England's capital. Her prophecy was fulfilled in a macabre fashion. The Prince of Cambria's head was mockingly draped with ivy leaves. Hopefully he slept on, unaware of that final indignity.

The
Monk's Curse

THERE is no evidence whatever to connect the comforting under-garment which bears his name, with that Long John of the 14th century who found monastic life a little tedious among the Benedictines of Little Malvern Priory. And certainly, in the unhappy experience which befell him, the comfort afforded by such underwear would have been of a very temporary nature. But the repercussions of the event and the legend arising from it have survived for the past 600 years. Dr Grindrod, a Malvern practitioner, early this century researched the story, weaving around it his novel *The Shadow of the Raggedstone*.

It seems that Long John derived rather less satisfaction from the enclosed life than did his brethren. For him the beauties of the surrounding hills above the valley of the Severn at Malvern Chase proved more uplifting. W. S. Williams, a Worcester writer, in his *Legends of the Severn Valley* paints a beguiling picture of what he suspects to have transpired on a summer day when the monk wandered alone over the hillside. In a glade carpeted with anemones and bluebells, the chestnut curls of a country maiden introduced an unexpected touch of colour as she paddled her pretty feet in a woodland pool.

Long John took in this vision, and returned to his austere home hugging only the memory of it to his breast. But on a subsequent occasion he encountered a different lady of more mature charms. She has been named in one record of the legend as the White Witch of Welland. No shyness inhibited this lady. She soon had the bashful monk under her spell. Her reputation for witchcraft, she protested, stemmed only from her medical knowledge and herbal skills. In those days, when bread and meat were the staple diet, herbal treatment, combined with the pure spring waters of Malvern and the dark syrupy concoctions of mingled fruits, sufficed to meet the needs of many ills and chills. She was, she convinced Long John, no witch – merely a 'wise woman' whose powers were exaggerated by local superstition.

Wise or not, she invited the bemused brother to her home, which was modestly furnished with a few stools, the inevitable cooking pots, a grey blanket or two, and a heap of sweet, fresh bracken for a bed. The monk became easier in his mind when she assured him, with a somewhat roguish twinkle in her eye, that she had ministered to various needs among others of his community – and was not unknown to the prior himself!

Whether on this or some subsequent occasion, the time soon came when Long John lingered too long in this inviting atmosphere. Matters came to a head one disastrous morning when his soberly clad brethren rose for morning devotions. The monk's absence was discovered, and with grave consequences. Brought before the stern prior, the hapless offender confessed all, bringing upon himself the unbridled wrath of his superior and the considerable apprehension of his fellows. The miscreant was reminded of a recent directive from the Bishop of Worcester that no man unaccompanied, or without a sound reason, was allowed beyond the priory boundaries. The spiritual fathers, it would seem, were not unaware of lurking dangers on the hills!

Long John was sentenced to perform an immediate and public penance. How he must have shrunk from the prior's tirade! A. R. Williams quotes it:

'Since you have behaved yourself as a beast, breaking out of holy precincts and seeking beastly pleasures, then, until I please, you shall be punished like a beast. I command that every day you will crawl like a four-footed hog from the foot of Raggedstone Hill to the summit, and there say prayers for your forgiveness!'

'Take him away!' the prior commanded Long John's fellow monks, and he was led to the foot of the curiously shaped Raggedstone Hill at the southern end of the Malvern range to begin his penance.

The Ward Lock Guide to Malvern ascribes the name of the hill to the small blocks of syenite spread freely over the surface. How anyone could scramble over these, as well as brambles, nettles, gorse bushes and other obstacles defies the imagination. Under the conditions imposed it called for a superhuman effort which might have been more endurable if the poor victim had faced a fixed sentence. Long John's ordeal went on day after day without a hope of respite from the implacable prior.

Finally Long John could stand no more. On what was destined to be his final cruel ascent he glanced upwards in despair. The summit of the hill formed a circular cone shape, divided off at the top into two jagged peaks, one a little higher than the other. The sun was sinking in the west and the despairing monk glimpsed a stange, long shadow resembling a heavy cloud emerging between the two peaks, throwing a dark column down the hillside to the foot of the valley below. Somehow he staggered over the last few yards and struggled to his feet, clutching his now ragged, heavy, dew-soaked habit around him, and threw hope and caution to the winds. Under a darkening sky pierced by lightning flashes and the crash of thunder, shaking with fever, he looked his last over the river below and the Cotswold hills beyond it.

'I will say no more prayers today,' he declared, 'I lay instead my curse upon my punishers. May all upon whom the shadow of this rock falls die before their time, as I do!'

With this he fell to his death in the valley below and was not seen again.

But his story lives on. Those who studied the odd shaped hill concluded that the shadow which appeared at certain intervals was not the normal, predictable consequence of the sun setting behind the two-peaked summit. It was, they pointed out, a kind of shrouding mist, a grey, hovering mantle which appeared at irregular times, independent of the position of the overhead sun.

For many years following the sad plunge of Long John, there were gloomy tales of the fate of some who passed through the shadow on the lower slopes of Raggedstone Hill. Among them were some whose names have gone down into history, overshadowed indeed with a grievous destiny. The Duke of Clarence, Richard III, one of Henry VIII's ill-omened queens, and other less prominent names have all subscribed, each in turn, by coincidence or by sad association, to the melancholy legend of the Curse on Raggedstone Hill.

A
Baronial
Bishop

TODAY we might find it hard to recognise the suitability of a comfort-loving man, with affluent tastes, for the vocation of the Church, since the Gospel story is centred around the lowly Nazarene.

No such incongruity would have occurred to Godfrey Giffard, who was appointed Bishop of Worcester in 1268. He came from a wealthy family in the ranks of the nobility, but it was not surprising that he aspired to the priesthood. The clerics of his day wielded considerable power, not only over their own subordinates in church, priory and monastery, but in the community at large. In the secular world, as well as the spiritual, they sat in judgment on their fellows. Bishop Giffard was therefore a man of considerable prestige. Whenever he set out upon a journey, and certainly when his purpose was to administer justice in the civil courts, he was escorted by a mounted procession of at least a hundred men.

His several residences were impressive, too. The Bishop's Palace situated in the walled garden adjacent to the cathedral was much used for ceremonial occasions, receiving prestigious visitors to the city, entertaining royalty, and so on. He also built two large houses on the perimeter of the city which were put to good use, and where he often wined and dined his guests. But it is probable that Hartlebury Castle was equally a home to him, if not his favourite one. He was a lover of country life.

The Hartlebury Castle of Bishop Giffard's day was much more impressive than the present bishop's home. It must have been extensively rebuilt when he moved into it. Its appearance was exactly like any baronial castle of that day, complete with fortifications and a surrounding moat. Its defences had been left incomplete by the previous bishop, so the newcomer made this work his priority. The castle was an important place of refuge and a main line of defence against the Welsh in border skirmishes.

Soon after Godfrey's appointment, King Edward I came to spend three days with him and to put down yet another rebellion from over the border. Letters were despatched to all men of influence, bishops, abbots, landed gentry and magnates of the realm who were in the area. The Bishop of Worcester was by far the biggest landowner in the county and had control over seven religious establishments, six knights and a dozen gentlemen in his diocese. The Bishop summoned them all to the aid of the King and the campaign against the Welsh was successful. King and Bishop parted in complete accord.

This may have led Bishop Godfrey, who loved hunting, to assume he had every right to enjoy the sport on Malvern Chase and in Feckenham Forest. But this was the king's prerogative. When Edward I came again to Worcestershire, he was highly indignant to find that local huntsmen had made free with his deer. He commanded an immediate enquiry, pressing it with the utmost vigour. It must have been disquieting for the King to find that his host, the Bishop, was the chief offender! However, the Bishop escaped with a fine of 500 marks, though others went to prison!

It appears that Bishop Giffard was of an obstinate turn of mind. He quarrelled with the Abbot of Westminster over their joint administration of Malvern Priory. The monks complained that their prior had committed a serious crime, so the Bishop deposed him and gave the office to his own nephew, William de Wikewan. But the deposed prior appealed to the Abbot of

Westminster, who forthwith summoned the new prior, and a deputation of the complaining monks, to come before him. They did so, and without more ado the Abbot of Westminster had them clapped into prison and loaded with chains! Back at the priory the remaining monks locked themselves in, refusing to have their old prior back, and the Bishop of Worcester came to join them. They came to the point of near starvation before giving in and it took the combined efforts of King Edward, the Pope and the Archbishop of Canterbury to pour oil on troubled waters!

But the King by now knew the Bishop of Worcester well and came up with a splendid compromise in order to soothe his indignation. He persuaded him to surrender his jurisdiction over Malvern Priory, and to be recompensed with the manor of Knightwick. To some this appeared to be bribery, and at the very least an unauthorized surrendering of ancient bishopric rights, as a matter of expediency. But if by this means the King, the Pope and the Archbishop could then retire in peace, the former prior disappear from public gaze, the starving monks be rescued and the Bishop's nephew and fellow prisoners be released from their manacles, who shall judge the Bishop for consenting to give in and let the old prior back, whatever his sins? Besides which, the manor of Knightwick was a very pleasant prize!

Ironically, after all the dust had settled, the Abbot of Westminster decided (on his own authority, and no one else's) that the guilty prior was not, after all, a fit person to lead the worship of the brethren at Malvern Priory, and deposed him forthwith!

Godfrey Giffard continued in office for a further 14 years, though in the last two of them he was in poor health. Perhaps it was during that time that he designed his own stately sepulchre. It is obvious that he wished very much to leave his mark upon the city of Worcester. In fact, his name achieved its greatest notoriety among 20th century citizens by pure chance. When Worcester's priceless Lych Gate was demolished to make way for modern buildings and a big new hotel, the proprietors planned to name the hotel The Gainsborough. Great quantities of equipment were designed and ordered, including beautiful china in abundance, all inscribed with the letter 'G'. Then it was discovered that the name was already patented in the hotel industry! Consternation reigned until some dignitary of the cathedral – which is the focal point of this premier site – was consulted. Was there any personality of some mark in the long history of that venerable building whose name began with 'G'?

For no other reason than this accident of planning, the long dead prelate's name has become a landmark in central Worcester, where the Giffard Hotel holds a prominent and popular place.

Railway
Disaster!

BROMSGROVE claims to be 'a town with a railway history' and its reputation is well maintained by local steam train enthusiasts. An event which gave Bromsgrove a prominent place in Britain's railway history occurred in November 1840 and immortalized the names of two Bromsgrove working men.

Thomas Scaife and Joseph Rutherford grew up in exciting times. As schoolboys in Worcestershire they would have envied their contemporaries in the north of England where Stephenson's *Rocket* was built, followed by the opening of the first railroad in 1825 – the Liverpool to Manchester line.

For the two Bromsgrove lads it must have been frustrating that their county gave only a lukewarm reception to the advent of the railway. The area had been well served for years past by inland waterways. Understandably it was reluctant to exchange the quieter, beautiful, established routes on water for the clang of steel and iron.

But progress would not be denied and the door of opportunity swung open for Thomas and Joseph when the great manufacturing city of Birmingham, just over Worcestershire's northern border, struck its own response to the challenge and opportunity of the railroad. The Birmingham and Gloucester Railway Company was formed to provide a new gateway southwards and westwards to the Bristol Channel and world markets beyond. It took time and hard bargaining to gain grudging consent from Worcester's civic dignitaries to allow the rail track to be laid inside the county's western boundary via Bromsgrove. The two local lads were in their 20s when the new company commissioned its first locomotive and named it *The Bromsgrove*. By midsummer of 1840 the first section of the line had been laid and Thomas and Joseph achieved their ambition, joining the company as driver and fireman respectively.

Early hazards, as well as technical problems, had to be overcome by ingenuity and sheer hard work. Thomas Scaife was subsequently described in the company's records as an engineer as well as driver, so he would have been involved in combating early difficulties. It so happened that his area, just south of Bromsgrove, presented a serious problem. A steep gradient on the Lickey Hills (1 in 37) defied, for a time, all efforts to surmount it. Yet when the solution came, the ascent was achieved in an engagingly simple way. After leaving Bromsgrove station the train was halted at the foot of the gradient; two engines were moved into place behind it and they gently propelled it upwards until the summit was reached. The two 'bankers', as they became known in railway parlance, were not coupled to the ascending train, so once they had completed their task they dropped unobtrusively back down the track to Bromsgrove, leaving the train on the summit to rapidly accelerate to full steam ahead.

Perhaps it was such ingenious manoeuvres as this which gave the steam trains an almost human element. It could be this indefinable touch of personality which generated a sense of accord between footplate crew and the great, gasping monsters they drove. 'You and your fireman had to create the power to get the train going,' explained one driver, 'It became part of you.' Certainly in those early days of trial and error Tommy Scaife and Joe Rutherford would have savoured to the full that exhilarating moment when the bankers dropped away and they resumed full control on that challenging summit. The gradient was given the unpretentious name of The Lickey Incline. It is famous in railway history, and the run which includes it has been described as 'the most fascinating in the nation's network.'

RAILWAY DISASTER!

In the summer of 1840 the line between Cheltenham and Bromsgrove was officially opened, providing two journeys each way on weekdays, though none at all on Sundays. A smooth routine was soon established. The morning train pulled into Bromsgrove at 10.50, achieved a five-minute turn-around and was back in Cheltenham by 12.27 – a highly satisfactory morning's work, followed by the lunch break and the afternoon trip. Passengers began to abandon the stage-coach, especially for long journeys. They found the train to be more comfortable and faster. Like the stagecoach the train offered three classes. First class seats gave full shelter from the elements, second class had no window glass and the cheapest seats were the most exposed, as were the 'outside' ones on the stagecoach.

In November of that year the extension of the line to Gloucester was opened. The company's objective was realised – it was indeed The Birmingham and Gloucester Railway. Prosperity was assured. Investment flowed in, and the future offered great prospects to the enterprising pioneers and their first employees. Joseph Rutherford got early promotion as 'foreman of locomotives.'

Then, six days later, on 10th November, disaster struck. At the close of an uneventful working day, shortly before six o'clock Tommy Scaife jumped on to the cab of an engine (ironically, it was named *The Surprise*) to talk to its driver, as it stood over an ashpit at the station. Joe Rutherford joined the group, which included the fireman, a stoker and a brakesman. Suddenly, without the slightest hint or warning, the boiler of *The Surprise* blew up with a terrific explosion! Tommy Scaife took the full force of the blast and was killed instantly, his body hurled more than 25 yards away. Joe Rutherford was projected through the surrounding brass rails and thrown a distance of many yards, only to die next day of scalds. The others survived the blast with injuries of varying severity.

The force of the explosion hurled the chimney 100 yards away according to E. G. Barnes, author of *The Rise of the Midland Railway*, and 'the top of the furnace was thrown clean over the station, behind which it finally embedded itself in a bank.' It was a disaster of major proportions. The engine was reduced to 33 cwt of scrap metal.

Long deliberation and many technical arguments faced the inquest jury two weeks later and their verdict placed the blame on certain iron plates of the boiler being of insufficient thickness. Many tributes were paid to the two Bromsgrove men who lost their lives so tragically. 'Thomas Scaife . . . a young man of excellent character and abilities . . .' reported Berrow's *Worcester Journal*, while the exceptional popularity of Joe Rutherford 'in the eyes of his subordinates and the Board' was emphasised by avowing that 'the men almost idolized him'. An immediate 'whip round' for his wife and three young children brought generous responses.

The two friends were laid side by side in Bromsgrove churchyard. On the tombstone, beneath the chiselled outline of a locomotive, is a lament full of pathos, yet reflecting again that mysterious sense of identification between man and machine to which many drivers testify.

> 'My engine now is cold and still,
> No water does my boiler fill;
> My coke affords its flame no more,
> My days of usefulness are o'er;
> My wheels deny their noted speed
> No more my guiding hand they heed:
> My whistle, too, has lost its tone,
> Its shrill and thrilling sounds are gone;
> My valves are now thrown open wide,
> My flanges all refuse to guide;
> My clacks also, though once so strong,
> Refuse to aid the busy throng;
> No more I feel each urging breath –
> My steam is now condensed in death.
> Life's railway's o'er, each station's past,
> In death I'm stopped, and rest at last.
> Farewell, dear friends, and cease to weep
> In Christ I'm safe, in Him I sleep.'

RAILWAY DISASTER!

It was a melancholy end to the exciting romance with steam of two popular, capable young men who died in their prime on the threshold of great progress in England. Mourners were not limited to the hundreds who knew them personally, who respected, loved and even idolized the young pioneers. In the world beyond their locality thousands of excited new travellers must have been halted in their tracks at the stark reminder that progress exacts a fearful price. But the names of Thomas Scaife and James Rutherford have survived in railway history and live again in a new song presented in February 1988 by Ralph Barton in Bromsgrove Museum.

> 'Lickey Bank . . . Lickey Bank . . .
> a million hearts sank
> the day that Tommy died.
> They laid him to rest on the high hill crest
> with his fireman by his side.'

The
Water
Curers

IN the late afternoon of an autumn day in 1842, a family group of three adults and three children climbed stiffly down from the Malvern stagecoach, retrieved their personal luggage from the coachman, and took possession of Holyrood House in the Wells Road. Furniture and household goods had arrived before them, and this day marked a new beginning in the lives of them all. In the 30 years which were to follow the arrival of 35 year old Dr James Manby Gully great changes would be experienced in Malvern, though they would not be welcomed by all.

Dr Gully's friend and colleague, Dr James Wilson, had some time before been on the Continent seeking relief from increasing ill health, and had returned excitedly claiming that his restoration, and that of many others, had come as a result of the Water Cure at Grafenberg. Its efficacy, he declared, had been established by over 700 publications since the days of Hippocrates, but had never received serious consideration in England.

Dr Gully was soon persuaded and the two friends had scanned a map of Britain, then taken train and coach to Malvern where Dr Wilson began immediately to enthuse upon the charms of what he saw to be the ideal location for the first Hydropathic Clinic. He fully agreed with the unknown poet who had left on record his conviction that:

'There is not in the wide world a valley so sweet
As the Vale in whose bosom the bright waters meet'.

Malvern waters had already attracted some fame, though, in actual fact, the 'bright waters' did not then meet. They were contained in the seven waterholes (wells and springs) which had survived the flood of prehistoric days, when Malvern was one vast lake and everything was submerged except the tips of the nine mile range of hills. As the waters subsided they left behind the gravelly soil which was ideal for forestry and, later, the wonderful diversity of flowering plants through the year's changing seasons. Daffodils, primroses, violets, blue-bells, yellow 'flags', marsh marigolds, dwarf broom, harebells, dog roses, autumn crocus and meadow saffron delighted the eye and perfumed the air freely and in abundance by the 19th century.

There was nowhere in England a better site, argued Dr Wilson. History had already proved its wells and springs to be Malvern's main attraction. Around them legends and rhymes had sprung. Healing virtues had been claimed for them. Bannister's *Breviary of the Eye* published in 1622, quoted this curious little verse:

'A little more I'll of their curying telle,
How they can help sore eyes with a new found welle;
Greate speech of Malvern Hills was late reported,
Unto which spring people in troops resorted.'

Dr Gully was by now equally enthusiastic. There was room, the friends decided, for two such establishments to be launched in the same year. Suitable premises were sought there and then.

Dr Wilson's establishment was soon functioning in Belle Vue Terrace in a refurbished hotel which he had renamed Grafenberg House, with what he described as 'the first ten or twelve anxious and hesitating patients'. Dr Gully opened a second property as a clinic and the two doctors collaborated closely, publishing various treatises and brochures jointly. Success followed, despite some opposition from other professional men, and Dr Wilson purchased a large site on which to build premises to house more than 60 patients, in addition to out-patients who boarded elsewhere. Dr Gully moved his family into The Priory in steep Church Street, freeing two more houses for patients and their clinic.

For Dr Gully it was not only the material success of the Water Cure which he enjoyed in those years. He gained much pleasure in receiving famous and interesting personalities as patients, his particular interest being literary men. His first such delight was in receiving the poet Alfred Tennyson. Politicians and other men with interesting roles in life roamed the hills with the doctor, and the increasing numbers of visitors subscribed in no small degree to Malvern's prosperity. By an Act of Parliament in 1851 it became a town.

In that same year there came a visitor to Malvern, ostensibly a patient seeking the Cure, but in reality a Bristol journalist named John Leech in search of a story. Unhappily for Dr Wilson, it was to his establishment that Leech applied and was accepted. He then proceeded to write a fascinating revelation of the treatment inside the Cold Water Clinics entitled *Three Weeks in Wet Sheets, the Diary and Doings of a Moist Visitor to Malvern.* It was heavily laced with satire.

His day commenced, he reported, at 6 am when he was woken by his bath attendant, stripped and clasped inside a wet, cold winding sheet 'like a mummy in a roll of papyrus'. Pummelled and rubbed by the manservant until the sheet became a poultice, he was more than ready for his breakfast of tea, white bread, butter and black treacle.

Midday brought a second cold sheet tubbing, and another at five o'clock, which was the prelude to a Lamp Bath. A 20 inch high 'clothes horse' was erected around him as he sat, naked, on a wooden chair with a fretwork footstool placed before him. A tin container holding a lamp filled with spirits of wine was placed beneath his chair, a series of wet blankets were draped over the 'clothes horse' and drawn to his throat, forming something like a bell tent beneath his apprehensive head. When the lamp beneath his chair was lighted, heat rose swiftly around the seated figure.

'Sat like Pythagorus on a tripod,' writes Leech, 'I asked – was anybody ever burnt in the Lamp Bath?' He was only half reassured by the rejoinder 'Not in this Establishment, Sir, but ... in another..!' Visions of Ridley and Cranmer in their martyrdom were soon swamped by torrents of perspiration flowing from the patient's forehead and by the glass of cold water pressed to his lips. 'Take a few swallows, Sir, to prevent you boiling over . . .' Release came with another cold tubbing before the main meal of the day – boiled mutton, vegetables and milk pudding.

Leech and his companions had time to enjoy the pure Malvern air on the doctor's spacious lawns before queueing for a turn in the outdoor Douche Bath. This contrivance consisted of two overhead pipes through which 'water roared like a lion to its prey, striking the shoulders with a merciless bang.' Happily the journalist leaves us with a much more agreeable picture of the clinic patrons' morning ramble over the hills, regulation drinking cup in hand, reporting at each of the seven wells in turn. There the party leader with a long-handled saucepan, ladled out the measure of spring water to each one with reverential solemnity 'as though it were twenty port!' Long before the well-tasting round was concluded Leech was reminded, he says, of Old Weller's description of some tea party guests: 'They were a-wisibly swelling afore my eyes, Sir!'

The little book must have delighted critics of the Cold Water Cure, of which there were many among medical men. Its association with homeopathy (which was considered then, as often now, as 'fringe medicine') provided ammunition for detractors. This factor probably disturbed the Worcester doctor, Charles Hastings, who was deeply concerned about preserving the integrity of the profession. Hastings' condemnation in medical journals of 'quackery' and exploitation may not have been aimed at Doctors Wilson and Gully, who were both qualified practitioners, but Dr Wilson nevertheless took umbrage. He retaliated by publicly associating Dr Hastings with the demise of an ex-patient named Need whose epitaph in Great Malvern churchyard was plaintive and poignant:

> Pain was my portion
> And physic was my food;
> Groans was my devotion,
> And drugs done me no good.

Dr Gully did not involve himself in this battle of words in medical journals. He preferred to rely upon the success of the clinics and the approbation of distinguished people from all over England.

In time the two pioneer clinics were joined by others, some with alternative functions like Dr Grindrod's 'compressed air bath for the lung and chest treatment'. For more than 40 years they flourished and even after the fashion waned their influence remained. Malvern's reputation as a health spa was established. Both Gully and Wilson came, in time, to be recognised as Malvern's benefactors. After Dr Wilson's death in 1867 a public memorial was erected – a drinking fountain in Abbey Road – largely at the insistence of Dr Gully, who publicly proclaimed his friend to be the Water Cure pioneer in England.

Despite all the controversies and difficulties which faced the two Water Curers, the history of Malvern would have been the poorer without them and the wider attention they drew to Malvern waters. Today the spring water is enjoyed by rich and poor alike. Excursionists who scramble over the lower slopes of the Worcestershire Beacon have easy access to St Ann's Well. Thousands enjoy its produce at the little cafeteria there, while the present Queen of England travels nowhere in the world without a supply of bottled Malvern water for her consumption en route.

Rhymes
and
Remedies

THE name of St Catherine crops up frequently in Worcestershire churches and shrines, though the little martyred
princess died long ago and far away – in Alexandria in the
year AD 307, to be precise. During the 19th century St
Catherine's Day was celebrated on November 25th and was
rather sensibly combined with that of St Clement (also of
Alexandria) to justify giving children a whole day off from
lessons and chores. It became their annual custom in those
days to band together and roam the countryside begging for
apples. Their energy and expectations must have been considerable judged by the proposed route outlined in their
joyfully chanted rhyme:

'Astley, Areley, Denley, Shrawley, Hartlebury and Elmley,
Mitton, Torton, Titton, Charlton, Holt, Hallow and Grimley'.

Apparently, undaunted by weather or by distance, the
lively groups roamed the country lanes chanting various
versions of the appropriate carol:

> 'Catt'n and Clement comes year by year,
> Some of y'r apples and some of y'r beer;
> Some for Peter and some for Paul,
> Some for Him who made us all.

Peter was a good old man,
For his sake give us some,
Some of the best and none of the worst,
And God will send your souls to roost.
Up with the ladder and down with the can,
Give me red apples and I'll be gone.'

Hopefully there were plenty of indulgent farmers to enter into the spirit of the occasion. The county enjoys an abundance of apple orchards and Catt'n and Clement's Day was as good a time as any to celebrate an abundant harvest with charity, good humour and thanksgiving.

It is a cheering thought that one way or another, despite the hardness of the times, grinding poverty and the all too swift passing of youth, it was possible to abandon care and discipline to enjoy a nonsensical rhyme like this one, in high spirits and with congenial company. Perhaps there is nothing quite like a popular song or even a chanted rhyme to promote that feeling of common purpose. Worcestershire has its old favourites. This one:

'Crosspatch, draw the latch,
  Sit at the fire and spin;
Take a sup and drink it up
  And call your neighbours in'

is as good a welcome as one is likely to find anywhere. A circling ring of children could be encountered almost any day with

'Polly go round the sun,
  Polly go round the moon,
Polly go round the chimneypots
  On a Sunday afternoon'

though you could probably find her addressed as 'Sally' in as many places.

111

With what glee an innocent victim might be challenged in a school playground with

> 'Adam and Eve and Pinch-me
>   Went down to the river to bathe,
> Adam and Eve got drownded
>   And who do you think was saved?'

Niceties of grammar went by the board so long as the rhythm was maintained and the expected answer met with suitable action on the victim's person!

'Remember, remember, the fifth of November,
  Gunpowder, treason and plot...'

has special significance for the people of Worcestershire for the plot was hatched and set in motion in the heart of our county at Huddington Court. Here, too, some of the conspirators fled for refuge when routed and the tragic Lady Winter, wracked with anxiety, awaited them, scratching on a window pane with her diamond ring a despairing record of her vigil. The words 'No cark, no care', are still visible.

Country songs and chants such as the Maypole song:

> 'All around the Maypole we will trot,
>   See what a maypole we have got,
> Garlands above and garlands below
>   See what a pretty maypole we can show'

leave very little to the imagination, and even the popular harvest shout cannot have been the subject of great inspiration:

> 'Up, up, up Harvest Home,
>   We have sowed and we have mowed,
> And we have carried the last load home
>   Up! Up! Up! Up! Harvest Home'

but are reminiscent of simple joys and recurring seasons in the countryside.

Why was it I wonder that Worcestershire children were taught

'I do not love thee, Dr Fell,
The reason why I cannot tell'

for it is unlikely that any doctors were loved by the infant population. And since their visits cost five shillings each time, it is not surprising that some families swore by traditional 'cures' such as a skein of red silk around the neck for quinsy, or trying to cure warts by applying a black snail, which must afterwards be impaled on a thorn! A much pleasanter cure was to 'sell' the wart to some philanthropic person, though it is a surprise that a customer was ever forthcoming!

A number of quite different remedies were recommended for whooping cough. One was to take the sufferer to as great a height as possible, scale the Worcestershire Beacon, for instance, or (in more recent times) circle around Pitchcroft in an aeroplane. Others were to feed the patient a slice of bread which has been buried in the earth for 24 hours, to stand the patient so that he can catch the breath of a piebald horse, or to prod the patient through an arched bramble branch rooted at both ends. It must be true that dire diseases call for desperate remedies!

For nosebleed that skein of red silk round the neck is brought into play again. Can this old remedy have a superstitious connection with the Biblical story of Rahab the harlot, who was spared destruction by hanging a red cord from her window? Presumably all quaint remedies have some significance in fact or fiction. To rub a nettle sting with a dock leaf seems a very much more sensible act, though repeating the old chant

'Ettle, Ettle, 'ittle Dock
Dock sh'll 'ave a golden smock'

is presumably an optional extra. Today's sufferers from cramp may be surprised to know that laying their stockings across each other at the foot of the bed when retiring for the night might afford protection from that appalling discomfort . . ..

Lady Brilliana Harley, who appears to have lived in Worcestershire during the Civil War, recommended 'fiseake' for children who were 'cuttin their teathe', composed of 'scury grass pounded and strained with beare'. According to W. S. Symonds, author of *Hanley Castle*, a contemporary of Lady Brilliana was a Dr Gaston whose suggested remedy for curing corns was nothing if not logical:

'Nevere ware tite bootes'!

The House
of
Shadows

ON the day when the Birt family decided to pull down the
keep which had served them as a communal home and a
refuge against Welsh invaders for many years, it marked an
important turning point in the fortunes and status of these
stalwart settlers, proud of their Saxon blood. It was quite
early in the 1400s when they erected Birtsmorton Court, the
lovely manor house in the Worcestershire countryside at the
foot of the Malverns. It was, and is, a beautiful timbered
structure with over-hanging roofs and gables, surrounded by a
deep moat; a drawbridge leads across the water to two round
bastions and the archway which once framed the portcullis.
Two hundred acres of pasture land surrounded it.

By the standards of their day the first generation of Birts to
make this place home had every reason to be proud of it. The
large, lofty rooms, latticed windows with gleaming glass panes
and a vent in the roof to draw away the woodsmoke from the
great fireplace in the main hall, made it a home to enjoy and
to share – fit for kings! And so, in time, it was to prove. But not
for kings only. The secret hideout within the structure of the
house was also destined to play a role not many years hence.
Danger, fear, hardship and narrow-minded prejudice would
bring fugitives in desperate need to knock upon the portals of
Birtsmorton Court.

The first such refugee was almost certainly Sir John Old-castle. In his time he had been a good soldier and a friend of the reigning king, Henry V, but he became a follower of John Wycliffe who had translated the Bible into English. The church authorities persuaded the King to outlaw the Lollards, as Wycliffe's followers became known. They were hunted down without mercy.

Sir John Oldcastle was their leader after Wycliffe's death. He was distantly related to the Birts who, though not so openly, appear to have shared his views about church ritual and the superstitions which had grown around it. The Birts had built a church alongside their new home, as was custom-ary, and were genuinely God-fearing. They did not approve of the condemnation of the Lollards and the awful penalties exacted upon them. The secret place of refuge in their new home might well have been designed because of their sym-pathies.

During the four years in which Sir John Oldcastle was being hunted down, he found refuge at the Court and, when his pursuers got too close, resorted to the surrounding forest land and to a hermit's cave in the hills. But he was a doomed man. He died a martyr in the fires of Smithfield and his cruel fate brought to the minds of Birtsmorton folk the curious legend which had sprung up relating to nearby Raggedstone Hill. The dark, cloudy column which emerged very occasion-ally between the twin peaks on the summit and cast a long shadow in a direct line down the hillside into their valley, was supposed to be an ominous sign of disaster to any person who passed through it, or upon whom the shadow should fall. They conjectured that the hapless Sir John, in his frequent flights between Birtsmorton and the cave on the hillside, had passed within its shade at some time.

It was not until the end of the 15th century that the legend again featured in Birtsmorton life. King Edward IV had taken the throne from his rather weak but saintly uncle Henry VI, but Henry's wife, Queen Margaret, with her son the Prince Edward of Lancaster, was determined to try and win back the throne for her husband. At one point they passed through Birtsmorton and she probably stayed overnight at the Court. History records the failure of Queen Margaret's attempt and the tragic death of 18 year old Prince Edward, and it has been claimed that mother and son also walked through the path of the Raggedstone shadow to their disastrous rendezvous with Fate.

So Edward IV kept his throne for another twelve years. He would often have visited Birtsmorton during that time, as the royal hunting ground of Malvern Chase was near. There is a story, recorded by the eminent W. S. Symonds, that his elder son (also Edward) accompanied him when he was about 12 years old. On the way to the Chase they rode through a clearing at the foot of the hill just as the ominous shadow threw its dark column down the hill! King Edward died in the following April; the boy succeeded him, reigned for only two months and then disappeared, with his younger brother, into the Tower of London. They were the famous 'princes in the Tower' and their disappearance is an unsolved mystery that has itself cast a shadow over the English throne.

Within a short time of that episode a daughter of the Birts inherited the Court and was married to Sir Richard Nanfan, who brought further prestige to the manor house by his appointment as 'Esquire to the King's Body'. His was the privilege of dressing and undressing the king. According to a manual drawn up in the previous king's reign, this apparently humble appointment carried with it responsibility for sweetening the king's garments and sheets – 'to gadyr sweet floures, herbis and rotes to make them breathe most holesomely and delectable'. Such a personal and trusting relationship brought with it more and more stewardships of Worcestershire manors and Sir Richard Nanfan was appointed Keeper of various parks, lodges and warrens in the area surrounding his Malvern home.

The legend became associated with the Birtsmorton family in a more personal way when Sir Richard was approached one day by a representative of the monks at Little Malvern Priory.

The visitor claimed that Sir Richard, in establishing new boundary posts, had wrongfully encroached upon land belonging to the priory. The unrepentant owner of Birtsmorton is said to have shown an indifferent, almost contemptuous attitude, which was met by his monkish visitor with a stern warning that 'God's judgment would fall upon him!' Whereupon, according to J. W. Willis Bund in a paper to the Worcester Archaeological Society, Nanfan lost his temper and dared the monk to do his worst. This produced a retaliation in the form of a prophecy that 'whenever the shadow of the hill on which they stood should fall upon the house, the eldest son should die within a year, ere his prime.'

Within a year the eldest son was dead. Toward the end of the 16th century the unmarried heir lost his life. Another fell from his horse and died of his injuries. Then came the Civil War and Sir George Nanfan's heir fell on the battlefield. In the reign of Charles II the last male heir of the Nanfans fell victim to a duel fought in his lady-love's honour. How sad that his chivalry did not save him!

So, long after the Little Malvern Benedictines had passed into history, the Nanfan male line failed. In the 18th century the Court was inherited by Catherine Nanfan who, when 15 years old, married Richard Coote, MP for Droitwich. He became Earl of Bellomont and thereby hangs a very tangled tale.

While Countess Catherine remained at Birtsmorton, her husband was despatched to New England with instructions to stamp out piracy in the Atlantic. On the principle of 'set a thief to catch a thief' he recruited the notorious Captain Kidd. By raising capital among wealthy English friends, mainly Worcestershire gentry, Bellomont equipped Kidd with a privateer, with instructions to round up and bring back to New England all pirate ships. Kidd was very successful. The booty confiscated proved an excellent investment for the Worcestershire investors. Then Kidd became greedy, kept some profit for himself and finally returned to his old ways, robbing honest traders under the flag of Lord Bellomont and (by implication) the English Government! An outcry brought about Kidd's arrest and execution for piracy, and disgrace upon the investors. It almost brought about the downfall of the government which had sent Lord Bellomont to stamp out piracy.

Within four years of this sordid affair Bellomont returned to the peace of Birtsmorton Court. A sadder and wiser man? Actually a much richer one as it turned out. It seems that he may not have lived long to enjoy his prosperity because Catherine married again three times, but his heir inherited the Birtsmorton estate and nothing sensational appears to have emerged from the Court since that time. It lies peacefully at the foot of Raggedstone Hill, much of its former beauty and appearance having survived the test of time.

Perhaps even legends eventually rest in peace.

The
Miraculous
Flight

THE stone effigy of Sir John Attwood, 14th century knight, lies in Wolverley church, near Kidderminster. The church was built in the 18th century on the site of an earlier one, and Sir John's effigy survived the transfer into the new church, although it is not certain what happened to the fetters which used to hang over his tomb, and which form a very important feature in his story.

Sir John is said to have followed the Black Prince, son of Henry III, on a Crusade to the Holy Land. Unhappily for him and for the wife he left behind at Wolverley Hall, he was captured by the Saracens and thrown into a dungeon. No more was heard of him.

The plight of the waiting partner in such circumstances was described in a touching ballad called *The Watch of the Crusades* with suitable pathos:

> 'She sits in the eastern turret
> Of that castle rugged and grey,
> And ever her watch is eastward kept,
> Till the long day dies away;
> Till behind her dies the sunset,
> And darkness the fair view fills
> That she looks across from its English walls,
> To its circling English hills.'

But, of course, then as now life had to go on. There was an estate to be administered and children to be raised, and the legend tells of how a suitor came along after a proper lapse of time, when her absent lord might be presumed to have perished, to offer marriage and protection.

Just as she was about to yield to the offer, she was alarmed one morning by an extraordinary outburst from one of the milkmaids, who rushed back from her customary task in the meadow on the fringe of the estate. She had gone there, as usual, accompanied by the family's pet dog, when he had rushed ahead and begun barking excitedly over a dishevelled bundle lying in the grass. Apprehensively the girl had approached and stared down on what transpired to be an emaciated figure clad in little more than filthy rags, who was either insensible or sleeping. The extraordinary thing was that the dog, far from showing hostility, was affectionately fawning over the figure on the ground. Dropping her milkpail the girl ran and brought her mistress to the spot. Both were mystified when the figure moved and was seen to be heavily manacled.

As the 'stranger' awakened from his stupor he broke into an emotional greeting to the Lady of Wolverley, the wife from whom he had been parted so long! She stared unbelievingly at first, for his appearance was so unlike the brave, mounted knight who had ridden off to the wars that it took the production of a love token to convince her that this was indeed Sir John Attwood. On parting he had deposited with his wife one half of a gold ring, taking with him the matching piece which he now held forth in triumph.

The wedding of course was cancelled and the celebration turned into a welcome home for the master of the household. Friends and tenants gathered round the festive board to hear of the adventures which had befallen him. His account of the battles concluded with a description of the miserable plight in which he had found himself in the Saracen dungeon. His hardships were confirmed, of course, by his emaciated appearance and the heavy iron fetters which had bound him, and his listeners were not surprised to hear that the Soldier of the

Cross had prayed for deliverance in his extremity. The answer came in the form of an angel, he told them, who came apparently to soothe and comfort the captive. At that point he had lost consciousness and then, to his own astonishment and everyone else's, had awakened in his own meadow with the family hound noisily caressing him!

How did he get there? He seemed to have only a vague impression of moving through space, he said, though he added with some hesitation that now and again he had a momentary sensation of soft feathers brushing against his body. Was his bearer an angel? The gallant knight was too modest to claim that he was the subject of divine intervention and suggested instead that a swan had brought him through the air.

The happily restored knight lived out his life in peace and accord at Wolverley, marked by works of charity. He directed that when the time came for a memorial to be erected over the family tomb, this act of God's mercy should be commemorated by a swan being carved upon his tilting helmet. His faithful dog, the only creature to recognise him in his pitiable state, was also to be carved in marble to lie at his feet. The pasture land where he was found had become known as The Knight's Meadow and any income arising therefrom was directed to be used to meet the cost of someone 'keeping the irons polished' and showing them to all who would like to view them, and to wonder at this marvellous tale.

Broadway's Bibliomaniac

WHEN Thomas Phillipps, a highly successful calico merchant, looked for a home in which to enjoy early retirement, it was to the lovely village of Broadway, on Worcestershire's eastern boundary, that he came. For Thomas it was a return to childhood haunts, and he was well pleased with his purchase in 1796 when he moved into Middle Hill. This large 18th century house, perched on a wooded gradient overlooking the village, proved to be an absorbing passion to him and an ideal home for the little 4 year old son who settled there with him.

Since Thomas was a 56 year old bachelor, somewhat irascible in temperament, his obvious love for the child must have surprised his new neighbours. But he pursued his way, developing his gardens, fishponds and stabling, and later purchasing more land behind the house to include the Beacon Tower on the summit of the hill. He was quite indifferent to the opinions or interest of others and perhaps it was that disregard of normal proprieties which had made him decide against marriage, preferring to 'buy off' his child's mother as a condition of gaining sole custody.

The child bore his father's name and grew up in apparent content. During his schooldays he acquired his father's interest in books and manuscripts. This was to make young Thomas, in later years, owner of the most famous library in Europe and the world's greatest collector. His is a fascinating story.

While Thomas Junior was studying at University College, Oxford, he met and fell in love with Henrietta Molyneux. His father resolutely refused to consent to his marriage, or to make it financially possible for his son to embark on matrimony. Happily for the young lovers, the marriage was not long delayed. The elder Thomas died and Middle Hill passed into his son's possession, at least for his lifetime. The father's will decreed that the property must pass to the next of kin in each succeeding generation. Thomas, happily contemplating his union with Henrietta, was not concerned about what should happen in the next generation. He was free to marry, and had a home into which he could bring his bride. Henrietta, who had been somewhat embarrassed by the earlier delay, gladly consented and the marriage took place in London.

Henrietta's sister had meanwhile married into the family of the Duke of Beaufort. As the time for the coronation of George IV was at hand, an Honours List was being compiled, and the Duke was in a position to exercise some influence in that direction. Happily Thomas had joined the family at a propitious moment – a baronetcy was granted to him by His Majesty.

Lady Phillipps presented her husband with three daughters in the course of time and Sir Thomas developed his interest in the manuscript collection begun and inspired by his late father. He embarked on travels in Europe and beyond, where he located literary prizes of worldwide interest. His introductions to various publishing houses and distributors led him into the discovery that precious vellum documents, when they had served their initial purpose, were being discarded as waste, sold to goldbeaters or, worse still, being boiled down as glue! It became an absorbing passion with him to locate and rescue them. He returned home, from time to time, with many literary prizes, devoting time then to the study of valuable data relating to kings, abbeys, manors and landed families. Friendship with kindred spirits was an added pleasure.

An almost idyllic life, one might suppose . . . and had it not been that Thomas's thirst for literary items of all descriptions increased to a consuming passion, amounting finally to near mania, he might well have lived and died a truly happy man. But clouds gathered on the horizon when Phillipps's income of £6,000 a year from his estates would not meet his family commitments as well as match his growing appetite for filling his library. Printing, binding and other important sidelines which he developed added greatly to his expenditure. Bills mounted. Payment was long delayed. The immense amount of capital invested in books and manuscripts remained, of course, locked up in boxes and files stacked in profusion around Middle Hill and in the rooms at the foot of the Tower. Sir Thomas seemed unconcerned about the agitation of trades-people to whom he owed money; his intention was to pay them all when convenient. But not all of his creditors were prepared to wait patiently and at one stage Phillipps and two farm workers (one armed with a pole) intercepted the local tax collector as he approached the premises to demand payment, and felled him to the ground! As a result Phillipps's fellow magistrates at Broadway, more to their embarrassment than to his, sent him for trial. His subsequent fine left him unrepentant and caused his other creditors more concern than it did himself.

However, despite his mounting financial troubles, scores of visitors were attracted to Broadway to see the now famous collection, and to confer with him on literary matters. Many of them were like-minded, some holding good credentials in the scholastic world, and he offered them hospitality. The guests had to pick their way to bed through passages and corridors stacked with boxes of papers and documents several feet high – and even to sleep with various items stacked around them!

All in all, Sir Thomas Phillipps was to leave a considerable mark on the history of Broadway, but by far the greatest blot on his record locally must have been his treatment of his eldest daughter, also Henrietta. She had the misfortune to fall in love against his wishes with a young student called James Halliwell who was, for a time, one of Sir Thomas's proteges.

He came as a visitor to Middle Hill in February 1842 and subsequently proposed marriage to Henrietta. Her father refused even to consider the match; his financial situation prevented him from providing the dowry which custom and conscience dictated. His hope was for his daughters to marry suitors capable of adding to the family fortunes. History was repeating itself, and despite the remembrance of his own romance being jeopardised on similar grounds, Sir Thomas remained adamant. But by August of that year Henrietta had come of age, accepted James and married him in Broadway church.

Despite her several appealing overtures, Sir Thomas never forgave his daughter and was filled with chagrin because, under the entail placed on the property by the terms of his own father's will, Middle Hill would eventually pass to Henrietta and James Halliwell. He resolved to rob the couple and their heirs of any future benefit on their inheritance.

In 1863 Phillipps looked for larger premises for his ever-growing library in Cheltenham and rented Thirlstane House there. It took him nine months to complete the move. During this period the tenant farmer entrusted with the gigantic operation transported 133 waggon loads, suffering collapsed wheels and broken axles as his carts lurched across the Cotswolds. Though much of the huge consignment was of great value, other books and documents were worthless, for the baronet had hoarded every newspaper he read, every letter and bill received and, indeed, any scrap of paper with writing on it!

In the ten years which followed, Sir Thomas was still in control of Middle Hill, though not living there. It was legally his for his lifetime, and he not only kept it vacant, but he systematically robbed and destroyed what he could of it. Lawyers prevented him stripping the lead from the roof and selling stoves, pipes and other fittings, but could not deter him from felling great numbers of trees including the beautiful mile-long avenue leading up to Beacon Tower. These he sold

127

for timber for £23,000. The whole estate sank under neglect and neighbouring farmers observed cattle wandering freely through ground floor rooms.

When Sir Thomas died in 1872 his estate was valued at £120,000, though the library eventually fetched several times that figure when split up and sold off by grandchildren (other than the Halliwells) who could not cope with it. Middle Hill was almost beyond repair when it came to the Halliwells. Legally it was theirs for life but it was beyond their financial resources to halt the decay, let alone restore it. It was a huge burden on their shoulders, as it would have been to their son later, but the law was more merciful than Sir Thomas had been. Recognising their impossible situation, the entail preventing the Halliwells from selling their inheritance was broken. Middle Hill and the Tower were sold to the Flowers family of Stratford-on-Avon for £80,000.

So the Phillipps family saga came to an end in Broadway, except for the villagers' mixed memories of the astonishing man who once declared 'I wish to have one copy of every book in the world'!